Stretching Students' Vocabulary

Best Practices for Building the Rich Vocabulary Students Need to Achieve in Reading, Writing, and the Content Areas

BY KAREN BROMLEY

SCHOLASTIC
PROFESSIONAL BOOKS

NEW YORK • TORONTO • LONDON • AUCKLAND • SYDNEY
MEXICO CITY • NEW DELHI • HONG KONG • BUENOS AIRES

For S. and C.

who love paper and continue to help

with the paperclips.

◆ ◆ ◆ ◆

ACKNOWLEDGMENTS

This book grew from the work of many teachers who willingly shared their "best" practice vocabulary teaching strategies and students who allowed their work to be included. I would especially like to thank Janet LaBare for her Web site ideas. I'm also grateful to Ray Coutu for his thoughtful questions and helpful suggestions, and to Wendy Murray and Terry Cooper for their support and encouragement.

Cover photograph by Jimmy Levine
Cover design by Vitomir Zarkovic
Interior design by Kathy Massaro

ISBN 0-439-28839-8
Copyright © 2002 by Karen Bromley
All rights reserved.
Printed in U.S.A.

1 2 3 4 5 6 7 8 9 10   40   09 07 06 05 04 03 02 01

Contents

Introduction

A **RICH VOCABULARY IS KEY TO LEARNING.** It can boost students' comprehension, improve achievement, enhance communication, and shape thinking. This book explores word-learning strategies for grades 3 to 8. You'll find many teacher-tested, research-based ideas for helping all kinds of learners build rich vocabularies. But this is much more than an activity book. As you read, you will gain a better understanding of the benefits and pitfalls of vocabulary teaching, and of effective word-learning practices based on using context, word structure, word origins, and language cueing systems. These practices will help you be a better teacher not only of vocabulary for reading and writing, but also for science, social studies, math, and other content areas. By carrying out the vocabulary-stretching strategies here, you will guide students toward becoming independent word learners, able to function successfully in school and the world.

How Words Are Learned

◆ **A** TYPICAL SCHOOL-AGED CHILD'S VOCABULARY
grows at a rate of three to 20 new words a day (Beck & McKeown, 1991) or between 3,000 and 7,000 new words a year. So, why do some students learn three words a day and some 20? There are many reasons, including the child's exposure to print and literacy experiences at home and in school; his or her family values, structure, and interactions; and his or her socioeconomic situation, culture, learning style, oral-language ability, and confidence level. Ten-year-old Lakeisha, for example, acquires new words easily and has a large vocabulary. In her home, the daily newspaper, books, magazines, two computers, and a college-educated mother provide literacy experiences. However, Mary Beth, one of Lakeisha's classmates, has trouble learning words. There are few books and no computers at home; her literacy experiences are watching television and talking to her siblings and parents.

Like Lakeisha and Mary Beth, your students probably learn words at varying degrees of difficulty and speed. Many factors affect vocabulary learning, among them exposure to print, literacy and language at home and in school, prior knowledge and background experiences, family values and interactions, socio-economic situation, culture, learning style, oral language, and confidence or shyness.

We know that children come to school with vocabularies that vary in size and that they learn at different rates for various reasons. For example, between grades 1 and 3, the vocabularies of children who live in poverty increase by 3,500 words a year while the vocabularies of middle-class students increase by 5,000 words a year (White, Graves, & Slater, 1989). And the vocabulary sizes of students who are considered disadvantaged are half to two-thirds that of their middle-class peers to begin with. Of course, other things like listening to someone read, shared storybook reading, and the type and amount of language at home affect vocabulary growth just as strikingly. The strategies in this book will help you reach all kinds of students. But, before I present them, let's explore why word learning is important in the first place.

Benefits of Word Learning

There are many benefits of studying vocabulary at all grade levels. Words are at the foundation of learning. They are key to establishing meaning in text. We need them to think and express ideas—to read, write, listen, and speak—throughout life. Wise teachers realize that a large vocabulary:

◎ **Boosts Comprehension** Word knowledge contributes greatly to comprehension, by some estimates as much as 80 percent. We know that a large vocabulary deepens students' experiences with books and authors, and makes it easier for them to infer the meaning of unfamiliar words they encounter in print, conversations, radio, movies, and the Internet.

◎ **Improves Achievement** Students with large, rich vocabularies score higher on achievement tests than students with small vocabularies. Also, because vocabulary is directly related to knowledge of concepts, having a large vocabulary enables students to achieve higher standards in school and, later, at work.

◎ **Enhances Communication** A large vocabulary promotes precise, powerful, and interesting speaking and writing. When students have a treasure trove of words at their command, they can understand others' ideas more easily and deeply, and others can understand their ideas more effectively as well.

◎ **Shapes Thinking** Words are tools for analyzing, inferring, evaluating, and reasoning. For example, students who know and can apply the grammar terms *noun*, *verb*, and *adjective* are more likely to be able to discuss and revise their writing to make it clearer and more interesting for others. Understanding terms such as *file*, *clip art*, *zip drive*, *chat room*, and *toolbar* gives students the tools to think about, and function in, a rapidly changing virtual world.

I encourage you to share these benefits with students to give purpose to their vocabulary work—to help them understand how a strong vocabulary helps them in school and in the work world. Parents need to understand these benefits, too, since parents are their children's first teachers and can be huge assets as you teach vocabulary and word-learning strategies.

There Is No "Best Method"

There is no one "best method" for teaching vocabulary, but we do know a few things about what strategies work best. For example, an analysis of 60 vocabulary studies done in kindergarten through college showed that using many repetitions of the same information about a word has mixed effects on reading comprehension (Stahl & Fairbanks, 1986). Conversely, one or two repetitions of a word's definition aren't effective either. However, strategies that are effective are those that include some repetition of definitions and the use of context—that actively engage students in meaningful learning (Beck & McKeown, 1991; Nagy, 1988).

Just as there is no single best method for teaching vocabulary, there is no best method for learning vocabulary. In fact, students vary tremendously in the ways they learn. Many teachers categorize learning into one or more of these modes:

◎ **visual** (sight)

◎ **auditory** (hearing)

◎ **kinesthetic** (movement)

◎ **tactile** (touch)

If teachers embrace all of these modes, they are more likely to reach all their students. In his theory of multiple intelligences, Howard Gardner (2000) expands this notion and identifies nine avenues or ways we learn:

◎ **verbal/linguistic** (learning from spoken and print language)

◎ **visual/spatial** (learning with shapes, patterns, diagrams, drawing)

◎ **musical/rhythmical** (learning with rhythm, rhymes)

◎ **logical/mathematics** (learning with lists, outlines, graphic organizers)

◎ **intrapersonal** (learning by thinking and reflecting individually)

◎ **interpersonal** (learning with and from others)

◎ **bodily/kinesthetic** (learning through movement and physical gestures)

◎ **naturalistic** (learning from the environment)

◎ **existential** (learning by questioning)

It is important to remember that neither adults nor children possess intelligence that is "fixed" in one area. Our tendency to rely on different areas in different ways, depending on the situation, has huge implications for teaching. For example, it is a mistake to assume that a student lacks linguistic potential (and, as such, ignore that area of learning) because she has logical/mathematical strengths, or to provide a musical child with many more opportunities to develop that skill while disregarding the interpersonal area because he may be shy. To function successfully in most situations, students must possess and apply skills in several areas. Since children learn in many ways, and since these ways of learning change and evolve over time, we need to be cautious about narrow teaching.

Gardner's theory has implications for vocabulary instruction, too. Traditional methods are designed for verbal-linguistic learners like Lakeisha.

The best word teaching, however, acknowledges the many ways students learn. For example, students like Mary Beth may respond better to approaches that include physical movement and gestures (bodily/kinesthetic intelligence) or music and rhythm (musical/rhythmical intelligence). To reach every student, then, you need to apply several types of strategies when you teach new words.

A good way to introduce those strategies to students is to tell them that learning words is like making friends. You would have a hard time recalling the name of someone you've met only once. You may remember the name and know something about someone you've met a few times. But, you can easily remember the name of a best friend because you know him or her so well. Tell students to think about word learning along those lines, on a continuum from "Don't Know" at one end to "Know Well" at the other. Then provide many different experiences with a word to ensure successful learning for all. Later, I will show you how.

A Model for Word Learning

I've found that four underlying assumptions guide successful word learning:

◎ **It is personal.** Successful word learning is different for each individual. Learners vary in terms of how they learn and what they know, greatly influencing what they learn.

◎ **It is active.** Successful word learning requires students to manipulate information by thinking, talking, or writing to make knowledge their own.

◎ **It is flexible.** Successful word learning may occur easily, without much effort on your part or the student's, or it may require intense, direct instruction. It may include one, several, or all of the recursive methods noted in the rings of the figure on page 10.

◎ **It is strategic.** Successful word learning happens when learners use a variety of strategies, depending on the new word and the situation. Conscious use of a strategy, process, or way of learning new words helps students become independent.

Attaching meaning to a new word is at the heart of learning it. Meaning often comes from the word's context which can be, among other things, the sentence or paragraph in which the word appears; for example, "*Photosynthesis* is the making of food in green plants from carbon dioxide and water in the presence of light." Context can also mean gestures and voice intonations that give clues to a word's meaning.

Meaning can be acquired without context, from a glossary, dictionary, or from analysis of the word's structure. For example, *photo* means "light" and

A model of word learning ▶

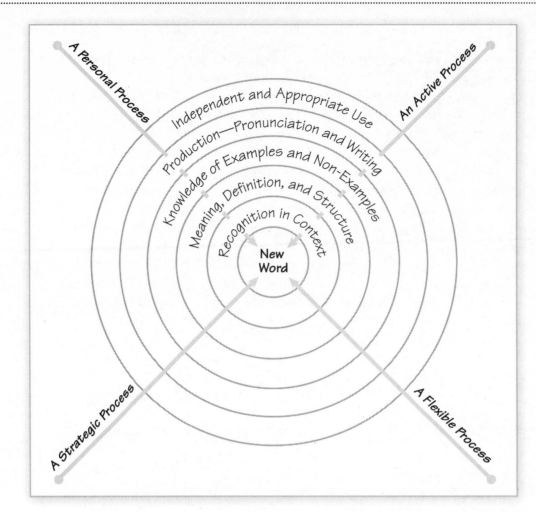

A Personal Process

An Active Process

Independent and Appropriate Use

Production—Pronunciation and Writing

Knowledge of Examples and Non-Examples

Meaning, Definition, and Structure

Recognition in Context

New Word

A Strategic Process

A Flexible Process

synthesis means "production," thus "production by light." Being exposed to examples of the word, non-examples, synonyms, antonyms, and related words, such as *chlorophyll*, can lead to more sophisticated word knowledge. Pronouncing, writing, and spelling a word can also guide students toward becoming more familiar and comfortable with its meaning. Finally, using the word independently and consistently in appropriate ways is the ultimate demonstration of successful word learning.

These ways of learning a new word are recursive; students don't necessarily follow them in order. Some students may move back and forth among them and may need to employ only one or two, until they can use a word independently. For example, a third grader may meet the word *photosynthesis* in his science book only once, and infer its meaning from context, before he "owns" the word. Without direct instruction, this student may be able to provide a non-example of *photosynthesis*. And, he may also be able to use the word appropriately in his science report or use it independently in a discussion. Other students, however, may need to experience the word in different ways and to different degrees before they learn it. For example, another third grader may need to see concrete examples of green leaves engaged in *photosynthesis*, look up the word's meaning in a glossary or dictionary, and receive systematic instruction in analyzing the structure of *photosynthesis* before he understands what it means.

Guidelines for Teaching Vocabulary

As you plan lessons and activities to teach new words, consider following these nine guidelines that grew out of the model you just read about. And consider the teacher-contributed ideas that support them.

Nine Guidelines for Teaching Vocabulary

- Connect Prior Knowledge
- Share Metacognitive Knowledge
- Actively Engage Students in a Variety of Ways
- Create a Word-Rich Environment
- Don't Fall Into the "Pre-Teaching Vocabulary" Trap
- Apply Strategies Across the Curriculum
- Teach Strategies for Independence
- Share Benefits of Word Learning
- Don't Forget Mnemonics

Connect Prior Knowledge

Simply repeating a new word isn't enough to help students like Lakeisha and Mary Beth learn it. Instead, it's important to tap into their personal schema, the prior knowledge they have stored in their long-term memories (Rumelhart, 1980). This means connecting the word to—or differentiating it from—what they already know (Rumelhart & Norman, 1981). For example, Lakeisha may link the unfamiliar word "traverse" to www.travelocity.com on the Internet, where she and her mother get airline tickets. She may differentiate it from "travois," the term for the pole and hide carrier used by Native Americans to transport belongings behind a horse. Mary Beth may not immediately connect "traverse" to anything and may, therefore, need a nudge to make a connection to a word she already knows, such as "travel." When students link new information to existing schema, the learning "sticks" because it has personal meaning. Here are two ideas to help build on your students' schema:

- **Vocabulary Anchors** (especially good for verbal/linguistic, visual/spatial, and logical learning) is a graphic strategy that helps students make connections between concepts that are new to them and concepts they already know (Winters, 2001). It is especially helpful to struggling readers and ESL students who may have problems with technical vocabulary in science and social studies. To introduce Vocabulary Anchors, show students a photo or drawing of a boat at rest in calm water and talk about how a boat can drift away if it doesn't have an anchor. (See Appendix, page 118.) Then, explain how we come to understand something new by "anchoring" it to something we already know. Now, show students what you mean:

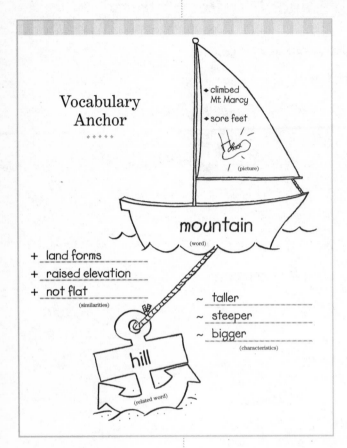

Vocabulary Anchor

◆ climbed Mt. Marcy

◆ sore feet

(picture)

mountain
(word)

+ land forms
+ raised elevation
+ not flat
(similarities)

~ taller
~ steeper
~ bigger
(characteristics)

hill
(related word)

▲

A Vocabulary Anchor for "mountain"

- Draw a simple boat and write a term on it your students probably know, like *mountain*.

- Choose a related word, such as *hill*, that students probably also know and write it inside a rectangular anchor under the boat.

- Connect the boat and anchor with a line to represent the rope.

- Talk about similarities between the words and write them below to the left of the anchor, keying them with a plus sign (+).

- Talk about the characteristics that set the words apart and list them below the box to the right, keying them with a tilde sign (~).

- Discuss a memorable experience you associate with the main word.

- Add a sail to the top of the boat and list a few key words or draw pictures to represent your memory.

- Summarize by reviewing the drawing and talking about what the words mean and why they cannot be used interchangeably.

Now lead students, as a class, through the construction of a few Vocabulary Anchors for difficult words you have pre-selected that they will encounter in their next science or social studies unit. Creating these anchors together allows students to share their experiences and prior knowledge as they build schemas for the new words. Students might complete Vocabulary Anchors you have partially constructed for them as they read, then share their work in small groups or with the class.

◎ **Picture Walk Words** (especially good for visual, interpersonal, and intrapersonal learning) connect students' prior knowledge to a new story, and, in the process, help them learn new words. Choose a picture book to read aloud. Before reading, introduce it by talking about the cover illustration and asking children to predict what the story may be about. Continue to encourage the children to predict as you take a "picture walk" through the book by looking at each page together without reading the text. As students talk about what may be happening in the story, they share their prior knowledge with one another. Through this discussion they begin to learn and use new vocabulary naturally.

Share Metacognitive Knowledge

Metacognition is our awareness of our thinking process and our understandings about how we learn. We use metacognitive strategies to monitor and adjust the way we process information. Sharing these strategies is a powerful way to help students learn words. When you model your strategies for figuring out and learning words, and when students share their ways of doing the same, they begin to take ownership of their learning and apply what they know themselves.

Use this reproducible list of metacognitive strategies as a bookmark so that students use them as they read.

◎ **Fix-Up Strategies** (especially good for verbal/linguistic, visual/spatial, intrapersonal, and logical learning) are visual tools to help students unlock a new word's meaning without immediately asking for help. (See chart right.) Each symbol stands for a metacognitive strategy that you can model for students, using an unfamiliar word from a text. Reproduce this list to create bookmarks, handouts, or a wall chart for easy reference.

◎ **Think-Aloud** (especially good for intra-personal learning) is a strategy many teachers use at all grade levels to articulate their processes for learning (Davey, 1983; Oster, 2001), by using language such as "Here's what I do…" or "That word makes me think of…." You can use think-alouds in whole-class and small-group lessons, in one-on-one conferences with students, and in informal conversations with groups of any size.

Many teachers also encourage students to think aloud with each other. Eight-year-old Zack recently told his classmates, for example, "When I came to 'pronouncement,' I didn't know what it meant, so I looked hard at its parts. I thought it looked like 'announcement' because the 'a' and the 'pro' are the only things different. I know what an announcement is and that meaning made sense in the sentence." As Zack explains the way he learns a new word, he teaches his classmates about strategies they might want to try.

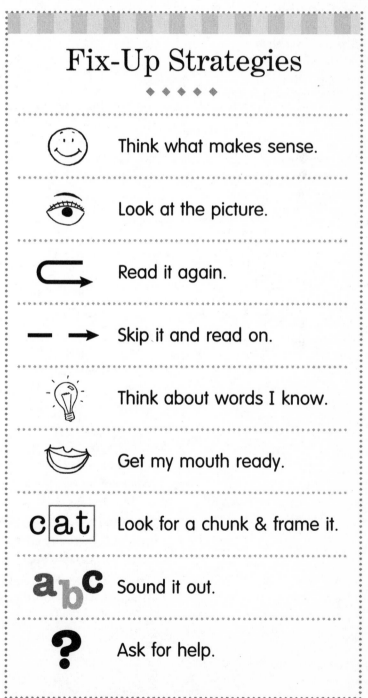

Fix-Up Strategies

* Think what makes sense.
* Look at the picture.
* Read it again.
* Skip it and read on.
* Think about words I know.
* Get my mouth ready.
* c a t Look for a chunk & frame it.
* abc Sound it out.
* ? Ask for help.

Actively Engage Students in a Variety of Ways

You will be a more effective vocabulary teacher if you plan lessons that provide varied opportunities for students to work with and use words. Help students manipulate words, talk about them, encounter them in a variety of contexts, explore their various dimensions, compare and contrast them, and justify their use. Here are three ideas that tap into different ways of learning:

◎ **Vo-back-ulary** (especially good for interpersonal, intrapersonal, bodily/kinesthetic, and verbal/linguistic learning) is a strategy Kristen Haglund, a special education teacher, uses to reinforce science and social studies vocabulary that is particularly difficult for her students. Kristen lists new words on the chalkboard and writes each one on a 5 x 8" index card. Then, she pronounces each word and explains its meaning. Next, she tapes one of the index cards to a student's back without revealing the word to that student. The student turns around to show the word to the whole class. She then calls on her classmates, one by one, for clues to help her guess the word. Kristen always reminds students to give clues that provide good information about the word's meaning, but don't give the word away; for example, for the word *penguin*, she might suggest:

◆ "It lives where it's cold."
◆ "It is black and white."
◆ "It has a beak."
◆ "Mothers and fathers take turns sitting on the eggs."

Clues unrelated to the word's meaning, such as "It has five letters," "It starts with a B," or "It rhymes with…," are unacceptable. Kristen always encourages clue givers to think about what they already know about the word, modeling as necessary.

With her classmates' clues and list of words on the board, the student tries to figure out which word is taped to her back. Once she guesses correctly, she chooses the next student, and Kristen repeats the process until only one word is left.

"Vo-back-ulary" is a powerful activity because it focuses on word meanings, encourages communication and cooperation, and requires students to use their background knowledge. Kristen says, "My students remember new vocabulary because they connect their own meaningful clues to the words. They have a lot of fun with Vo-back-ulary, and beg to play it every day."

◎ **Start Friday With a Song** (especially good for musical/rhythmical, verbal/linguistic, and interpersonal learning) is an activity that helps students, particularly ESL learners and struggling readers, learn words and the rules of English in a motivating and fun way.

Each Friday Sharon Bieber, Kathy Grabowski, Jane Kintz, and Ann Marie Zevotek's classes get together in the auditorium to start the day with song. The teachers plan the songs and lessons on a monthly basis, and take turns teaching each Friday. To prepare, a teacher writes the song lyrics on chart paper for everyone to see.

Before singing, the teacher leads students in a shared reading and discussion of the song. For example, "Which Witch Is Which?," a tune from a Winnie the Pooh recording by Phil Baron and Richard Friedman, is used to introduce homophones. The teacher points out the use of punctuation, capitalization, rhyming words, and special vocabulary in the lyrics. Student volunteers show classmates special vocabulary and punctuation that appears in the song. Later, in their individual classrooms, teachers have students work in pairs to explore the concepts further, for example, by making a class "Homophone Book." Each page of the book contains a pair of homophones that the children illustrate and use in a sentence.

The teachers also use this activity for teaching content-area words. For example, songs such as "Clouds" and "What Is Matter?" by Suzy Gazlay (*The Mailbox*, 2000) reinforce learning about weather. During a unit on animal classification, students sang songs such as "Habitat" by Bill Oliver and "Food Webs and Chains" by S. Kitchen (*The Mailbox*, 2000). Each class then chose a classification and composed songs about it, using facts they learned in their studies of animals.

These teachers also use the book *101 Science Poems and Songs for Young Learners* by Meish Goldish (1999) as a source of curriculum-related poems. They say their students look forward eagerly to "Start Friday With a Song." They believe it not only improves word learning, but also reinforces important concepts and builds a sense of community among students.

Songs

Reptiles
(Sung to "London Bridge")

Reptiles have rough, dry skin,
  Rough, dry skin,
  Rough, dry skin.
Reptiles have rough, dry skin
And most are harmless.

Reptiles lay eggs with hard shells
  Eggs with hard shells,
  Eggs with hard shells.
Reptiles lay eggs with hard shells
And are cold blooded.

Some have shells and some have scales,
  Shells and scales,
  Shells and scales.
Some have shells and some have scales.
They are reptiles.

Fish
(Sung to "Twinkle, Twinkle Little Star")

Chorus:
Bubble bubble under water,
How I wonder what fish are.

Using gills to help them breathe,
Instead of lungs like you and me.

(Repeat Chorus)

Using fins to help them swim,
In the light or when it's dim.

(Repeat Chorus)

Their body temperature changes with the flow,
It changes with water wherever they go.

(Repeat Chorus)

Mammals
(Sung to "Three Blind Mice")

What are mammals?
They have fur or hair.
They nurse their young.
They're born alive.

They run, hop, swim, climb
And one even flies.

They are mammals.
They are mammals.

Birds
(Sung to "Are You Sleeping?")

What are birds?
What are birds?

Their bodies are covered with feathers.
Their bodies are covered with feathers.

They have no teeth in their beaks.
They have no teeth in their beaks.

They hatch from eggs.
They hatch from eggs.

They can fly, swim and hop
Walk and run
Walk and run.

They are warm-blooded
And have a backbone.
They are birds.
They are birds.

◎ **Word Detectives** (especially good for verbal/linguistic, visual/spatial and logical/mathematical learning) is a strategy to introduce and extend understandings of new words. Using a graphic organizer and *Inspiration Version 6* (1999), a software program that provides a template for graphically representing a concept, students explore a single word in multiple ways. Graphic organizers show key ideas and information in an organized way (Bromley, DeVitis, & Modlo, 1995; DeVitis, Bromley, & Modlo, 1999).

Before starting this activity, be sure your students know that a synonym is a word that means the same thing and an antonym is a word that means the opposite. Then choose a target word, such as *enormous*, and enter it in the center box of an enlarged version of the organizer. (See sample below.) Enter words such as *huge*, *large*, and *gigantic* in the boxes connected to the "synonym" box. Enter words such as *small*, *tiny*, and *little* in the boxes connected to the "antonym" box. In the box under the target word, put "Things that are this" or "Such things as" and enter examples, such as the Empire State Building, Mt. Everest, and the Atlantic Ocean.

Next, have students carry out the activity independently by asking them to find their own target word and giving them a blank organizer. If necessary, you can adapt the organizer for struggling students. Here are some suggestions:

◆ Add symbols or pictures as students brainstorm ideas about the word.

◆ Simplify the organizer by including fewer symbols and, therefore, requiring less information.

◆ Change the words "synonym" and "antonym" to "opposite" and "similar."

A teacher's Word Detective organizer for "enormous," created with Inspiration *Version 6*

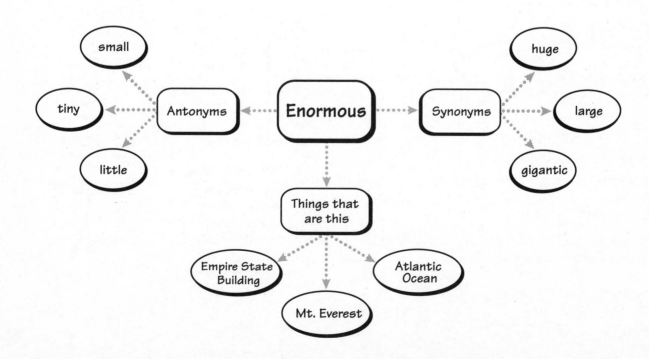

Internet Connection

www.inspiration.com

Inspiration.com is the site for Inspiration Software, an easy-to-use program for grades 4 to 12 that helps kids think and learn visually. The program includes clip-art symbols, templates, a www connection to download clips from the Internet, webs, and other diagrams. Download a free 30-day free trial for Mac or PC.

Dodie Ainslie (2001) extends this idea by having her fourth graders keep standard 4 x 6" spiral notebooks as "Detective Notebooks." In them, students maintain an ongoing list of "suspects," difficult words they encounter when they read. Next to each suspect, students write clues to its meaning, such as "The word is in…," "Its part of speech is…," or "A different word that contains part of this word is…."

Each week two students are assigned the job of "Lead Detective" for the class. They pick a word from one of their "suspect" lists and "brief" the class on it. To prepare for the "briefing," the two students make a graphic organizer showing the word, its definition, part of speech, the sentence from which it came, any other context clues, and a sentence they have written containing the word. (See sample below.) Then they make their organizer into an overhead transparency and show it to their fellow detectives, who take notes in their Detective Notebooks. Students are encouraged to ask questions about the "suspect," just as a detective would in an actual briefing; for example, "Does *awed* mean the same as *inspired*?" or "Could I use *awed* to describe my cat?" After the new word is shared, Dodie adds it to the word wall and often uses it as a "bonus word" for spelling.

Word Detectives is very popular in Dodie's classroom. Because of it, her students talk more and no longer shy away from unfamiliar words. Instead, as she says, "They attack them like seasoned professional detectives!"

A graphic organizer created by a fourth-grade Word Detective ▶

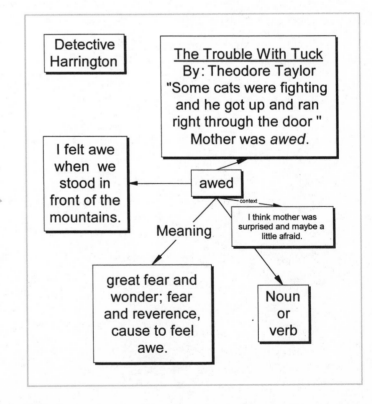

Create a Word-Rich Environment

Students absorb a lot of information from their surroundings and their interactions with others, perhaps even more than we realize. Look around your school and classroom, consider the opportunities for word learning by asking yourself these questions:

◎ How much print, including student writing, is visible?

◎ Is the writing of all students on display, not just of those with large vocabularies and those who learn words easily?

◎ Does my classroom library have books and other print materials at varying degrees of difficulty, so all students can read independently?

◎ Do I schedule time for vocabulary learning in each subject area?

◎ Do I have students talk in pairs, in small groups, and with the whole class regularly to build their oral fluency and confidence?

◎ Do I explore the origin and structure of words occasionally regardless of the age group or grade level I teach?

◎ Do I use interesting, powerful, and precise language and applaud students when they do the same?

You may notice many bare walls in your school. When you examine the schedule for a typical day, you may discover how little time is actually devoted to vocabulary instruction and paired or small-group learning. The project described next (Hurst, 2000) will help you create an environment that supports word learning.

Characters from A–Z can promote school-wide learning when you post charts like this outside your room.

◎ **Characters from A-Z** (especially good for verbal/linguistic, visual/spatial and interpersonal learning) can inspire students to read new books, revisit previously read books, use the library or Internet, and work together. Hang 26 blank charts on the walls around your room or in the hall outside your room.

◆ Write a letter of the alphabet at the top of each poster.

◆ Photocopy, scan, or have children draw pictures of various characters from well-known books, using one character for each letter of the alphabet.

A

1. Alexander from <u>Alexander and the Wind-Up Mouse</u>
2. Arthur from <u>Arthur's Valentine</u>
3. Arizona from <u>My Great Aunt Arizona</u>
4. Annie from <u>Annie and the Old One</u>
5. <u>Anansi the Spider</u>
6. <u>Amazing Grace</u>
7.
8.

- Paste each picture on the appropriate poster and add the character's name and title of the book.
- Encourage students to add characters and titles to the lists on an ongoing basis.

Alternatively, you can invite the entire school to participate by announcing that your class is having a contest open to all grades to identify familiar characters in books. You can:

- Make entry blanks available in the library, the principal's office, and your classroom. The entry blank should ask entrants to list the alphabet letter, name of the character, and title of the book.
- Have your children check entries and write them on appropriate posters.

The challenge might be to find 10 names (or even 20) for each poster. Q, X, and Z may be difficult. Encourage children to use many different sources to find names of main characters. You might even announce the most creative or unexpected resources. You can put your students in charge of the classroom or school project. Let them create an entry form or use the one below, and have them collect the entries and write in names and book titles on the posters. Let your students visit the alphabet lists daily in pairs to practice reading vocabulary together by reading entries to each other. At the end of the project, have your students take down the posters, punch holes in each one and make an alphabet "big" book using metal rings so they can continue to enjoy the project in the classroom. The big book can also be signed out and taken home for your students' families to enjoy or borrowed by another classroom to read.

Entry form for Characters from A–Z ▶

"Characters from A–Z"
◆ ◆ ◆ Entry Form ◆ ◆ ◆

Alphabet Letter _____

Name of Character _____

Book Title _____

Source _____

Your Name _____

Don't Fall Into the "Pre-Teaching Vocabulary" Trap

Just as there is no best way to teach vocabulary, there is no best time to teach it either. So, be flexible. Vocabulary doesn't always need to be taught before your students begin studying a topic or reading a book that may contain unfamiliar words. You may just wind up wasting precious time teaching words they already know. As a rule of thumb, pre-teach a few difficult words that are central to the meaning of what is about to be learned. Then provide opportunities for students to meet new words—those that are not so central to meaning—and figure them out independently. If they have difficulty, offer support by giving them the unfamiliar word's pronunciation and meaning. You may also want to teach vocabulary after the reading session or study block, when you have a better idea of which words give the students trouble. Here is one idea to help students identify difficult words they need help with. You will find more ideas like this later in this book.

◎ **Newspaper Know-How** (especially good for verbal/linguistic, intrapersonal and bodily/kinesthetic learning) works at any grade level, but Patty Lyons uses it successfully with fourth graders. First, she gives pairs of students newspaper sections and highlighter pens. Then she has them find and mark five words they don't know. From there, she talks with them about the importance of learning new words to understand what is going on in the world, reviewing Fix-Up strategies similar to the ones discussed earlier in this chapter. (See page 13.)

Patty models the use of context, structure, and grammar to figure out one or more of the new words. For example, when a pair of students identified the word *dermatologist* in an article, Patty used the Think-Aloud strategy with them:

"Okay, the title might give me a clue: 'Experimental Cream May Help Fight Skin Cancer,' and here are two phrases, 'epidermis layer' and 'damaged cells' that tell me about the skin. The term 'derm' is in both *epidermis* and *dermatologist*, so maybe that means skin. Yes, the picture in the article shows layers of skin. Now, I know a biologist is a person who studies living things, and a zoologist is a person who studies animals, so maybe '-ist' means 'someone who.' So, that would mean a dermatologist is someone who studies the skin."

By thinking aloud, Patty shows her students how to apply word-learning strategies. She also gives students time to share their processes with one another. After modeling, she puts students in pairs and has them practice the strategy with one another so that they can hear how peers go about figuring out the meaning and pronunciation of new words.

You can extend Newspaper Know-How by having students tune in to television or radio news at home, listen for unknown words, and involve a family member in unlocking their meaning. They can then bring the new word to school to share with the class.

Apply Strategies Across the Curriculum

The application of knowledge is a true test of whether or not it has been learned. Students need to have opportunities to use the strategies in reading, science, social studies, math, health, music, and art, as they read trade books, textbooks, and other sources of information. Textbooks especially contain many multisyllabic words and technical vocabulary. Observing students reading them, therefore, can give you a good idea of who can apply word-learning knowledge and who is having trouble. The following three strategies, as well as those in the remaining chapters of this book, will help you guide your students to use their word-learning skills across content areas.

◉ **ABC Books** (especially good for verbal/linguistic, visual/spatial, intrapersonal, and interpersonal learning) aren't just for beginning readers. They can help you teach and reinforce important content-area concepts that might be difficult for some students to learn by more traditional methods. After studying matter, for example, Kristin Ignatz's fourth graders spend two to three science periods making a book they call *The ABCs of Matter*. Kristin says, "This helps children internalize vocabulary and concepts. It's a concrete way to understand abstract terms." (See sample page below.) Here's how to make an ABC book:

1. At the end of a unit of study, write key words on slips of paper and place them in a jar. Show students the filled jar and have them write the letters of the alphabet on a piece of paper, leaving a space under each letter. Challenge them to brainstorm and write down under the appropriate letters the words you have placed in the jar.

The D page from
The ABCs of Matter
▼

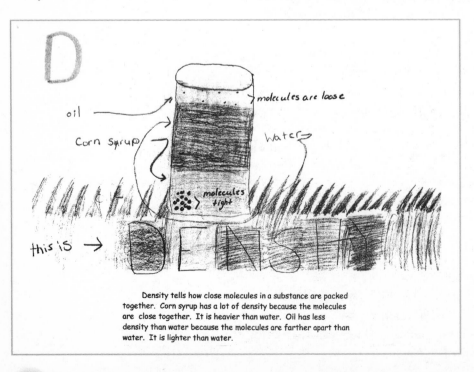

oil
molecules are loose
Corn Syrup
Water
molecules tight
this is →
DENSITY

Density tells how close molecules in a substance are packed together. Corn syrup has a lot of density because the molecules are close together. It is heavier than water. Oil has less density than water because the molecules are farther apart than water. It is lighter than water.

2. After five to ten minutes, have each student pair up to share and expand their word lists. If they have trouble, putting them into groups of four may give them more resources to work with.

3. As a class, share responses and record all the words alphabetically on chart paper or on the chalkboard. Then show students the words in the jar, compare them with the class lists, and fill in any gaps.

4. Tell students that, since they have learned so much about the subject, they are going to write a book. Pass the jar around and have each student choose a word without peeking. When everyone has selected and read his or her word, allow a few minutes of "think-time" for students to visualize the word and review its meaning using books or other classroom resources.

5. Have each student draw a picture illustrating the meaning of his or her word.

6. When the drawings are done, have students write a brief summary that defines the word and describes its importance to the unit. Students who finish early can choose another word from the jar.

The M page from The ABCs of the Iroquois

Kristin compiles the pages into a class book that students read together and keep as part of their classroom library. She says, "After creating this book, many students begin to use pictures as a means of learning vocabulary words independently."

For social studies, Ann Bernard reads *Turtle Island ABC: A Gathering of Native American Symbols* by Gerald Hausman (HarperCollins) to her fourth graders. The book focuses on differences among Indian groups and, as such, introduces her students to new terms related to Native American cultures. To reinforce these terms, Ann's class creates an ABC book based on the Iroquois.

First, Ann divides 26 blank sheets into nine sections, with a letter of the alphabet at the top of each sheet, and posts them around her classroom. She then has students move around the room, adding vocabulary words and colorful illustrations to each sheet. (See sample page above.) To fill in the boxes as thoroughly as possible, many of students reread the published books on Native Americans, which Ann makes available in the classroom, or search the Internet. When each letter page is full, Ann binds the book and the class reads it together. From there, it becomes a permanent addition to the reading corner.

Ann says, "Creating an ABC book gave my students an opportunity to construct their own vocabulary in a highly motivating way. The book was read so often it began to fall apart. The fact that they created it as a group gave them a great sense of community, ownership, and pride in their learning."

Internet Connection

www.surfnetkids.com/ dictionary.htm

This site contains descriptions and links to several online dictionaries for kids.

Teach Strategies for Independence

It's critical to teach students strategies for figuring out unknown words on their own. As you read further in this book, you will discover a variety of ways to help your students become word wise by using context, structure, letter clusters, letter chunks, and word origins. The ability to be a "word detective," "word solver," or "word wizard" gives a child independence from peers and adults. The next strategy builds independence in attacking unknown words.

◉ **SCUBA-D** (especially good for intrapersonal and verbal/linguistic learning) is a six-step metacognitive strategy (Salembier & Cheng, 1997). Students use the letters in "SCUBA-D" for figuring out unfamiliar words they encounter as they read. (See the chart on the next page.) Special education teacher Kristen Keuter's middle-grade students love SCUBA-D and have shown remarkable success using it.

To introduce the strategy, Kristen writes "SCUBA-D" on a chart and talks about what each letter stands for (**S**–Sound it out, **C**–Check the clues in the sentence, **U**–Use main idea and picture clues, **B**–Break words into parts, **A**–Ask for help, and **D**–Dive into the dictionary). Then she explains how the strategy can help in science, social studies, and other subject areas. From there, Kristen models SCUBA-D and students practice it together on new words. Kristen displays the SCUBA-D chart on a wall. She also has students make bookmarks, often with pictures of themselves in scuba-diving gear. Kristen says students with learning disabilities really connect with this strategy. It gives her struggling readers confidence by helping them be much more independent as they learn new words.

Share the Benefits of Learning Words

Help students understand that a large vocabulary is useful to them both inside school and out. Encourage them to use their word-solving strategies to unlock new and difficult vocabulary outside school. Here is an idea that can help you do that:

◉ **Find & Photograph** (especially good for verbal/linguistic, bodily/ kinesthetic, naturalistic and existential learning) is an idea Amy Litchfield adapted (Keller, 1999) to use with third graders. Find & Photograph requires students to search their environments for words.

Amy purchases several disposable cameras and sends them home with her students on weekends. Their mission is to find and photograph "survival words" on signs in the community that drivers, bikers, skateboarders, or walkers follow, for example, *stop, men working, hospital,*

(continued on page 26)

SCUBA-D

Stretching Students' Vocabulary   Scholastic Professional Books   •   An explanation of how to use this reproducible appears on page 24.

Sound it out

Look at the letters and say the sounds. Start at the beginning of the word and move to the end.

Check the clues in the sentence

Think about the meaning of the other words in the sentence. Guess a word that fits and that starts with the first letter of the unknown word.

Use main idea and picture clues

Ask yourself what the story is mostly about. Read the title and first sentence. Look at the pictures. Then guess the best word to fit.

Break words into parts

Look for smaller pieces or parts in the big word.

Ask for help

Ask your teacher or a friend for help.

Dive into the dictionary

Look the word up. Use the letters in parentheses next to the word to figure out what it sounds like.

Internet
Connection

**www.polaroid.com/
education/education.
jsp**

This is the site of the
Polaroid Education
Program, a good
resource for teachers
and parents. It contains
information about free
teaching workshops
and using photography
in the classroom.

**www.ncrtec.org/
picture.htm**

**www.classroom
clipart.com**

These sites contain
indexes of pictures for
the classroom, with
suggestions and
lessons for using them.

danger, *yield*, *exit*, and *enter*. The fact that many of her students are bikers and skateboarders is a great motivator.

After students have taken their photographs, Amy has the film developed. Then she has students write a caption report for each of their photos, explaining where they found the sign and what it means. Photos and caption reports are displayed in the classroom on a "Find & Photograph Survival Words" bulletin board. Amy says once students are familiar with survival words, they find them independently and bring them to class, along with other new words they discover in their environment on marquees and billboards.

This sign was on a trail. I saw it when I was walking with my Dad and my dog Dusty at the park. It said "WARNING" in big letters. My dad said it means we can't go swimming or climb on the rocks by the water. I didn't care because it was too cold to go swimming. The trail is scary when it gets close to the edge of the cliffs. I think the sign is to keep us safe.

Students learn survival words with Find & Photograph.

Don't Forget Mnemonics

Mnemonic devices (especially good for logical-mathematical and intrapersonal learning) aid and improve memory (Carney, Levin, & Levin, 1993). In fact, the phrase "mnemonic" comes from the name of the Greek goddess of memory, Mnemosyne. One kind of mnemonic device is a sentence in which each word begins with a letter in the target vocabulary word—for example, "Big elephants can always use some energy" for the word *because*. Mnemonics are so popular with Nancy Mangialetti's third graders that she keeps a "Mnemonic Chart" in her classroom that students create and refer to when they encounter troublesome words and concepts.

Encourage students to create their own mnemonics for difficult words. You might find that they remember how to spell words better if they make up the mnemonic than if you supply one for them.

Mnemonics to Remember

- **Because**—Big Elephants Can Always Use Some Energy.

- **Adidas**—All Day I Dream About Soccer.

- **Planets in order from the sun**—My Very Eager Mother Just Served Us Nine Pizzas (Mercury, Venus, Earth, Mars, Jupiter, Saturn, Uranus, Neptune, Pluto).

- **Directions in clockwise order**—Never Eat Slimy Worms (north, east, south, west).

- **Dessert**—Two s's since we usually love deSSert and want more. (A desert has only one s.)

- **Geography**—George Eats Old Gray Rats And Paints Houses Yellow.

- **Lines in the treble clef**—Every Good Boy Does Fine.

- **Spaces in the treble clef**—FACE

◆ ◆ ◆ ◆

SUMMARY

"The secret of a good memory is…forming diverse and multiple associations with every fact we care to retain." (James, 1890). When it comes to teaching children new words, this quote couldn't be more appropriate. The secret of good word learning is forming diverse and multiple associations with words. In this chapter you have read about some effective ideas for doing that in active ways. In subsequent chapters, you will learn about sound word-learning practices using the cueing systems of language, context, word structure, word origins, and the Internet.

2

Getting Started With Word Learning

NINE-YEAR-OLD AARON KNOWS THAT A WORD LIKE "LION" is a string of letters that go together in a special way to communicate meaning. But he may not know that *lion* is a basic unit stored in his memory. Along with the printed graphics, letter sounds, and word shape, Aaron's brain stores images and associations that add rich meaning to his concept of "lion."

Much of Aaron's schema (i.e., what he sees, hears, experiences, reads, or does in his life) is organized and stored in his long-term memory (Rumelhart, 1980). Aaron's schema for "lion" may include various visual images such as a stuffed toy he played with as a baby, a real lion he saw at the zoo, the Cowardly Lion in *The Wizard of Oz*, or an ad with a picture of a lion cub lying under a tree in Africa. Aaron may also have many associations that accompany each of these images. He may remember the color and feel of the fur on his toy lion; the yellow eyes, intimidating roar, switching tail, and smell of the real lion as he paced in his cage at the zoo; or the zebras and ocelot who also live on the African plains, which he learned about at school. Experiences and associations like these make "lion" a rich concept for Aaron.

Aaron's Word Knowledge

Aaron, like many children, first develops a large listening vocabulary made up of words he recognizes when others speak. Aaron's speaking vocabulary grows from his listening vocabulary and his own experiments with word-making as a toddler. His reading and writing vocabularies grow from his listening and speaking vocabularies, as well as from the instruction he receives in school and from vicarious or incidental experiences he has with words at home and in the world. (See figure below.)

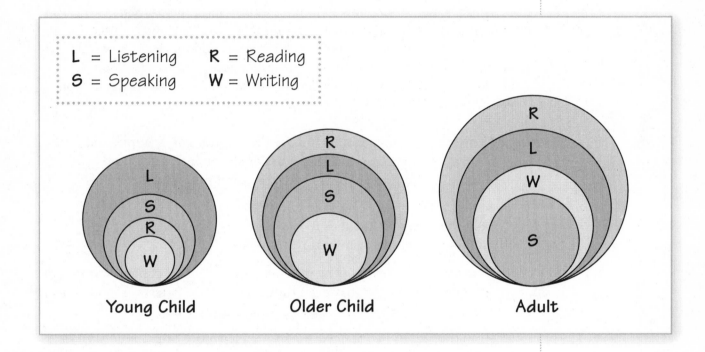

L = Listening   **R** = Reading
S = Speaking   **W** = Writing

Young Child   Older Child   Adult

Aaron has two types of vocabulary. His receptive vocabulary consists of the words he recognizes and understands when he listens and reads. His expressive vocabulary is the words he uses when he speaks and writes. Young children typically have larger receptive vocabularies than expressive vocabularies. But in the upper elementary grades, as children become more fluent, the sizes of their vocabularies change. For example, as a third grader, Aaron's writing vocabulary is his smallest vocabulary. But, by the time he is in high school, he will probably be able to use more and different words in writing than he uses when he speaks.

Since a big part of our jobs is to teach new words not only for language arts, but also for science, social studies, math, health, and other subject areas, there are some basic things to know about words. To begin, a word is "a series of letters that go together in a special way to communicate meaning." Every word has at least one:

All four vocabularies increase in size as children develop into adults. The relative size of each vocabulary changes over time as well.

◎ **Morpheme** or meaning unit. For example, "cat" is made up of one morpheme, "cat," while "cats" is made up of two morphemes, "cat" and "s" (plural for more than one cat).

◎ **Phoneme** or sound unit. For example, "a" has one phoneme, "uh," while "the" has two phonemes, "th" and "uh," and "cats" has three phonemes, "kh-ah-tz."

A word can possess many different associations and represent complex concepts. Some researchers believe that everything we have seen, experienced, read, or done in our lives is stored in long-term memory. The vocabulary challenge is in knowing how to retrieve from storage the concepts, associations, and images we possess and the words that stand for them.

To help students acquire rich, multidimensional knowledge of words, we need to be explicit in teaching about various aspects of words. Linguists identify four cueing systems students can use to unlock words the do not know (Weaver, 1994):

◎ **Semantics** The meanings attached to a word. For example, "cat" can mean a four-legged animal that purrs or a shortened version of "Caterpillar," a heavy vehicle that scoops and moves earth.

◎ **Syntax** The grammatical functions of a word. For example, "row" might be a verb (to use oars to move a boat) or a noun (a line of sunflower plants in a garden).

◎ **Grapho-phonemics** The print and sounds that represent a word. For example while "night" has five printed letters, two letters, "g" and "h," are silent and the word has three sounds or phonemes, "nh-i-tuh."

◎ **Pragmatics** The accepted ways to use a word. For example, a child may be called a special nickname by her parents, such as "Pumpkin" or "Sweetie Pie." But she may not want you to use that nickname in school because it's not an appropriate in that setting.

Word-study activities that grow from these understandings about words can help students store and retrieve the graphics, sounds, images, associations, and uses connected to new words and the concepts for which they stand. When students know a word, and the many dimensions of that word, they can more easily understand and use the word. They will probably be better thinkers, talkers, and listeners because of that knowledge. Their comprehension of spoken language and written text will be much better, too. So, as teachers, we have the challenge of helping students:

◎ Build large vocabularies that are rich with images and associations.

◎ Acquire independent word-learning strategies for life-long use.

Pitfalls of Current Vocabulary Practice

Unfortunately, studies of what teachers believe about vocabulary—how it is acquired and how it is best taught—raise many questions. As you consider these pitfalls, think about how you teach new words and answer the reflection questions.

Narrow Views and Teacher Control of Vocabulary

Many teachers have a one-dimensional view of the purpose of vocabulary instruction. Watts (1995) found that fifth- and sixth-grade teachers wanted only to help students understand what they were about to read. The teachers did not see the broader benefits of teaching vocabulary, such as improved achievement in school, better communication skills, and enhanced thinking ability throughout life. Nor did these teachers vary their methods. Typically, they defined a word for students, asked students for a definition, and gave a short context for a word. Observations showed these teachers controlled the talk about word meanings and followed the basal reader closely.

QUESTIONS FOR REFLECTION

◎ **What do I believe about word learning?**

◎ **Do I have a narrow or broad view of the role of vocabulary?**

◎ **Do I always follow the same procedure when I introduce new words?**

◎ **Who does the talking about new words?**

Overreliance on Basal Reading Series

Teachers often introduce words their students already know, often using mechanical methods. Ryder and Graves (1994) studied fourth- and fifth-grade basal reading series, and students and teachers who used them. They found instruction in basals was neither "rich nor deep." Words were consistently introduced by the teacher, who gave a definition, used the word in a sentence, and then directed a discussion on some aspect of the word. Students did not have opportunities to "...manipulate words in rich and varied ways, to discuss words and their relationships, and to explore and justify the relationships and associations they discover," and already knew many of the words targeted for instruction. The researchers concluded that basal instruction is not powerful enough to improve comprehension of new words in context.

QUESTIONS FOR REFLECTION

◎ What is my view of the relationship between words and comprehension?

◎ Do my students already know the new words the basal says I should teach?

◎ Which words do I feel are key to their comprehension?

◎ Do I vary my vocabulary introductions? How?

◎ Do students talk about the new words and their definitions?

◎ How do I involve students in manipulating and comparing new words?

Low-Level Activities in Textbooks

Textbooks tend to include traditional, low-level vocabulary activities that are not supported by research. Harmon, Hedrick, and Fox (2000) looked at teachers' editions of fourth- to eighth-grade social studies textbooks, for example, and found activities focused on definitions, matching terms, and fill-in-the-blanks. Many activities appeared in review sections of chapters or units where words were not introduced first. There were no suggestions for helping students manipulate word meanings at the higher cognitive levels needed to understand and remember them.

QUESTIONS FOR REFLECTION

- Which specific words are key to my students' comprehension of concepts?
- Do I vary the ways I teach new words? How?
- Do students offer definitions and talk about the new words?
- How do I involve students in examining, manipulating, and processing new words?

Mindless Practice and Little Engagement

Engaging students in activities that are meaningful is most effective. Stahl and Fairbanks (1986) found that a word is learned not from repetition, but from many encounters with it in a variety of contexts over time. Practice with flash cards may improve sight-word recognition, but to gain complex, multifaceted knowledge of a word, a student needs many meaningful and different experiences with it over time. That way, he comes to know the word and its many dimensions well, and it becomes part of both his receptive and expressive vocabularies.

QUESTIONS FOR REFLECTION

- Do I provide activities that include more than repetitive practice?
- Do I provide practice with new words in context?
- Do I assume that, once taught, a word is learned?
- Do I engage my students in activities that are meaningful and fun? What are some of them?

Incomplete Definitions

Dictionary definitions often promote inadequate understandings of words. McKeown (1993) studied fifth graders' word learning and found that dictionaries define a word by using similar words that don't always give full meanings of the concepts the word stands for. McKeown revised these definitions to include ideas she considered central to a word's meaning, which resulted in richer responses from students. For example:

◎ **prudent**   (DICTIONARY) Planning carefully ahead of time; sensible; discreet
(REVISED) Thinking things over carefully *before making a decision*

◎ **improvise**   (DICTIONARY) To make, invent or arrange with whatever is on hand
(REVISED) To make *something you need* using whatever is available at the moment

Even with revised definitions, students' knowledge of the words was limited. Simply learning definitions was not a powerful route to vocabulary development. McKeown believes that to fully understand a word, students must have "…repeated exposures to information-rich contexts." It's therefore best to think of dictionary definitions as good introductions to word meanings, but only introductions—not routes to mastery of a word.

QUESTIONS FOR REFLECTION

◎ Do I rely on the dictionary to give my students accurate word meanings?

◎ Do we use the dictionary as a starting place to learn new words?

◎ Do I rely too heavily on synonyms to help my students learn new words?

◎ Do my students and I note previously learned words when we see them in new contexts?

Unreliable Context

Beck and McKeown (1991) and Rupley, Logan, and Nichols (1999) found that context could reveal a lot or a little about a word's meaning. Sometimes context does not contain enough clues; at other times it does contain clues, but students do not have the ability to use them effectively. Here's an example:

> Josh's bag was full of candy from Halloween. He took it to school and shared it with his friends on the playground. But, they all <u>deserted</u> him when it was gone.
>
> <u>Customarily</u>, the U'wa tribe abandons newborn twins in the forest or tosses them into rivers, believing they are ill equipped for life and bring bad luck.
>
> He struck the stone with a hammer and as the stone crumbled in two he saw the <u>impression</u> of a leaf that had fallen to earth thousands of years ago.

In the first example, the words *Halloween* and *candy* might lead a student to believe that *deserted* is related to *dessert*, since they conjure up thoughts of sweet things. Or a student might connect *deserted* to the word *gone*, and infer its meaning correctly. In the second example, there seem to be no clues to the meaning of *customarily*. And in the third example, the meaning of *impression* is not really clear, but *of a leaf* may suggest a picture or the shape. Context within a sentence or longer text, therefore, is not always reliable in helping to determine a word's meaning.

QUESTIONS FOR REFLECTION

- Do I assume context always gives my students the clues they need to figure out new words?
- Do I assume my students know how to use context to unlock a word's meaning?
- Do I have a rich understanding of what "context" means?
- How can I help my students use context to understand word meanings?

Sound Vocabulary Teaching
in Grades 3 to 8

Sound vocabulary teaching is based on many factors, including an understanding of the four cueing systems, or ways to process words, which help students acquire and comprehend language: semantics (meaning), syntax (grammar and usage), grapho- (print) phonemics (sounds), and pragmatics (setting and appropriateness). See page 30 for more information on the cueing systems.

Children learn a huge number of words simply by listening. They absorb and begin using words from conversations between adults, siblings, and peers, and when others speak and read to them. Children become aware of print in their environment in much the same way. Without being taught, many children learn words in meaningful contexts like signs and advertisements. For example, graphics and pragmatics help young children quickly learn to recognize the yellow "M" symbol for the word *MacDonald's* and the red hexagonal signifying *Stop*. Children who learn language easily seem to rely on the cueing systems intuitively to learn new words.

Often, a child's inaccurate use of a new word gives away the fact that she possesses incomplete knowledge or is not using all the cueing systems. For example, a seven-year-old shows incomplete semantic understanding and partial use of grapho-phonemics when she refers to the President's guards as the *secret circus* and her father's foot fungus as *Catholic's foot*. But through the seemingly passive activities of listening and reading, children absorb many, many new words and their meanings. This kind of casual or incidental learning of words occurs throughout one's lifetime.

Children also learn words that parents, adults, siblings, and peers teach them. This kind of direct or intentional learning happens all the time in school when, for example, teachers explicitly teach pre-selected words to prepare children for reading a textbook selection. It also occurs during reading when the teacher draws attention to a new word's meaning, structure, or use.

When intentional learning focuses on only one aspect of a word, it can result in incomplete word learning, as one first-grade teacher discovered. After playing the song "Clementine" for her students, and focusing on the phonemics only without the accompanying graphics, the teacher thought she had taught her students the words. However, when she heard some of them sing, "Oh, my darling Calvin Klein," she knew she needed to change something. The children hadn't attached the appropriate semantics or grapho-phonemics to the word *Clementine*. When she showed a picture of Clementine, displayed the song's lyrics, and focused attention on the words, the students realized *Clementine* was a woman. The teacher could point out that her name begins with a *Cl*, like *Clara*, the first name of one of the students in the class, and ends like *Stine*, the last name of another. So, it's important to provide many, rich intentional experiences involving the four cueing systems to help children become effective incidental word learners.

Sound vocabulary teaching is based on social-constructivist theories of learning (Dewey, 1938; Piaget, 1963; Vygotsky, 1978). In other words, when students construct meaning for themselves, it is more effective than having meanings imposed by someone else. Also, social interaction contributes significantly to students' ability to make meaning of words and text, because, when students interact, they extend and deepen their thinking. That's why so many of the strategies in this book require students to work in pairs and small groups.

The teaching practices described in the remainder of this chapter will get you started in helping students work cooperatively and begin using the cueing systems to learn new words. All the ideas come from real teachers who:

◎ Have a broad view of word learning that extends throughout the curriculum and beyond the classroom. They teach vocabulary in science, social studies, and other content areas, and they help students appreciate the English language.

◎ Don't always follow the teacher's manual. They make their own decisions about new words to teach. They involve students in those decisions and in how they will learn words.

◎ Know that definitions aren't enough. They have their students examine, process, paraphrase, and participate in meaningful activities to learn about the dimensions of a new word. They realize the importance of offering students many different ways to learn and remember words.

Now, consider the classroom practices of several teachers in grades 3 through 8 in relation to the pitfalls of vocabulary teaching and the four cueing systems you have just read about.

◎ **S2-D2: Spell, Say, Define, Draw** (especially good for verbal/linguistic, visual/spatial, and intrapersonal learning) is a strategy that encourages the use of all four cueing systems. Before or after reading a new selection in language arts, science, or social studies, Michele Mele identifies several key words. Then, she and her students discuss and research the words. They might, for example, paraphrase definitions found in a dictionary or glossary since this requires students to process a word's meaning using their own vocabulary. Then students choose at least two new words and explore them on their own in multiple ways by entering the S2-D2 information on a template. (See Appendix, page 119.) The sample on the next page shows Aaron's S2-D2 sheet for *cartography*. Michele says, "A picture is worth 1,000 words. Each symbol helps my students remember the new word. Drawing their own pictures also helps them make personal connections with new words."

Michele's students keep their S2-D2 sheets in binders, organized by subject area for easy reference. She often has students "pair" (two students) or "square" (four students) to share entries. She also makes time for students to reread entries and quiz each other on them.

Aaron's S2-D2 for "cartography" helps him remember the word. ▶

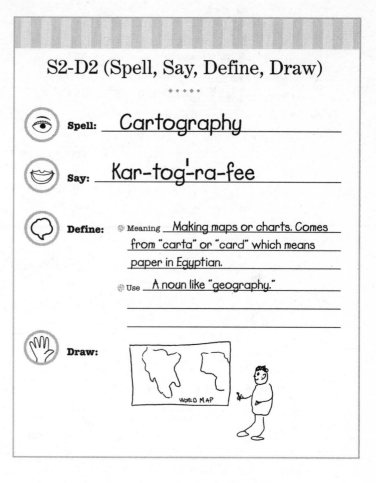

S2-D2 (Spell, Say, Define, Draw)

Spell: Cartography

Say: Kar-tog'-ra-fee

Define: ⊙ Meaning Making maps or charts. Comes from "carta" or "card" which means paper in Egyptian.

⊙ Use A noun like "geography."

Draw:

WORLD MAP

⊚ **Word Webs** (especially good for verbal/linguistic, visual/spatial, intrapersonal and interpersonal learning) use three of the four cueing systems: grapho-phonemics, semantics, and pragmatics. Word Webs are a type of graphic organizer (discussed in Chapter 1) that show key ideas and relationships in an organized way. They are effective tools for teaching and reinforcing vocabulary. Typically, teachers display only words that represent central ideas on a graphic organizer; since those ideas are isolated and highlighted, organizers can be especially helpful for struggling readers and ESL students. Many teachers create graphic organizers, or have their students create them, to introduce a new topic or review one they've covered.

Start by modeling how to create a Word Web. After reading a chapter in a textbook, write content-related words randomly on a chart or chalkboard. For example, from a science book you might choose:

◆ Igneous   ◆ Shale   ◆ Sedimentary
◆ Granite   ◆ Marble   ◆ Slate
◆ Basalt   ◆ Limestone   ◆ Rocks
◆ Gneiss   ◆ Metamorphic

Then organize words by isolating major categories, for example "types of rocks": *Igneous*, *Metamorphic*, and *Sedimentary*. Write these terms on the chalkboard. Next, think aloud about subcategories. For *shale*, for example, you might say: "I remember that shale is rock that is soft and forms in layers under the ocean," and write *shale* near *Sedimentary*. Continue thinking aloud and writing the names of objects near the category in which they belong, and then connect the boxes with lines and arrows to complete the Word Web. (See sample right.)

You can also have groups of students create Word Webs using the words from a news article on a timely topic, such as the hazards of ultraviolet rays. (See sample below.) First, print the important words and phrases on 3 x 5" cards and give them to a group of three or four students. Then have students arrange the words into main categories and subcategories. Finally, have them tape or glue the cards to tag board and add "connector words," such as *blocked by* between *ultraviolet rays* and *glass*, to show how the words relate to one another.

Ask students to share their webs with the class and explain the connections, using the correct vocabulary. During the discussion, you and your students may see alternate ways of fitting together the information. These discussions can help you assess how well students understand concepts, and indicate concepts you may need to review. Word Webs like these make good planning tools for writing, too.

Adding "connector words" to this Word Web makes relationships clear to students.

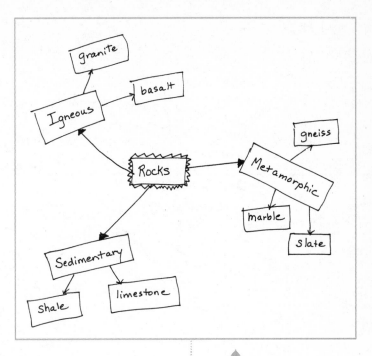

Creating Word Webs like this one helps students learn key science vocabulary and concepts.

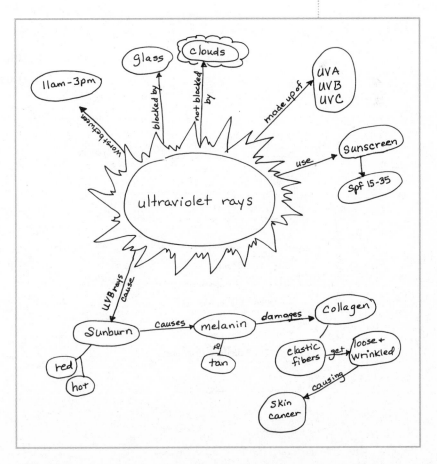

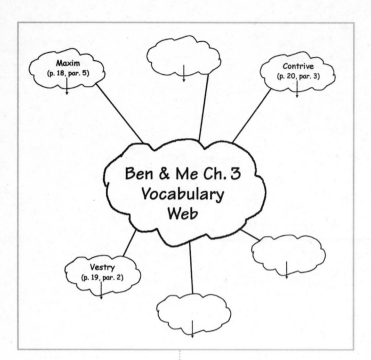

Teacher and student can select three new words to learn with this Word Web.

Stephen Ferraro uses Word Webs to help his fourth-grade students use context in learning word meanings. Typically, he selects three words he feels students need to know—for example, from *Ben and Me* by Robert Lawson (Little, Brown), a book they were reading in language arts, he chose *maxim, contrive,* and *vestry.* He asks students to find each word's meaning by "using the text to figure out the definitions." Students write down the meanings on a web that Stephen distributes, along with the pages and paragraphs where the words appear. (See sample left.) Stephen knows the importance of using context clues and semantics to arrive at a word's meaning. (In Chapter 3, you will find more ideas for using context to develop vocabulary.)

The Venn diagram is another type of graphic organizer that's useful for teaching vocabulary, even vocabulary other than English. For example, a teacher I know uses the Venn to have students compare and contrast English and Spanish words. First, students list English words and their Spanish counterparts in separate circles. Then the teacher has them draw boxes around letters and patterns that the words share, and note elements in the overlapping section to help them remember the meanings of the Spanish words. (See sample below.)

A student uses a Venn Diagram to compare English and Spanish words.

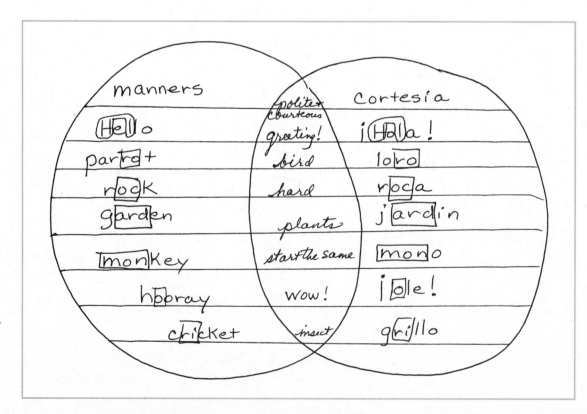

◎ **Concept Definition Maps** are another kind of graphic organizer that promote understanding of a word's many levels of meaning. They go beyond dictionary definitions and encourage the application of personal knowledge (Schwartz, 1988). You can use them to pre-teach difficult vocabulary at all grade levels, but intermediate- and middle-school students can use them on their own with great success. (See Appendix, page 120.)

Start by displaying a blank map on the overhead transparency and, in the center, write a familiar word such as *cheese*. (See sample below.) Ask for a definition of the word. A student might say, "a food that goes on pizza." Then think aloud as you supply the vocabulary terms to fit the boxes on the map. Be sure to discuss how you arrived at these terms and then write a new, more complete definition at the bottom of the map.

When students understand how to use the concept definition map, give them a new word from their science or social studies curriculum, and have them work in pairs to create their own maps. Encourage students to use information from the glossary, dictionary, and their own background knowledge. Then, using all their information, have them write a new definition that is fuller and more meaningful than one in the dictionary.

Once you've covered a few of these basic strategies, give students choices. They can do an S2-D2, a concept map, a Venn diagram, or a Word Web to keep in binders, organized by subject area. Regardless of the strategy, however, explanation, discussion, and sharing are critical to the successful use of graphic organizers.

This Concept Definition Map shows many aspects of the word "cheese." ▶

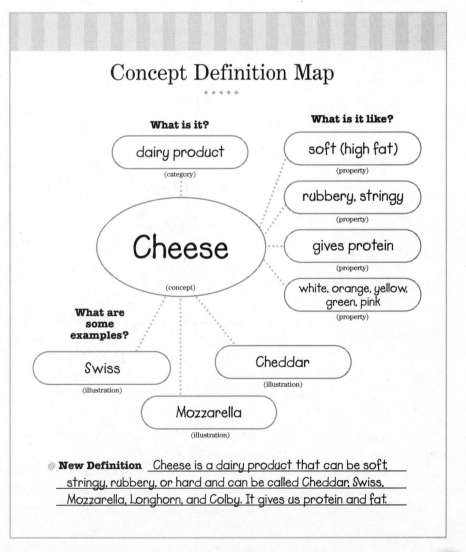

Concept Definition Map

What is it?
dairy product
(category)

What is it like?
soft (high fat)
(property)

rubbery, stringy
(property)

gives protein
(property)

white, orange, yellow, green, pink
(property)

Cheese
(concept)

What are some examples?
Swiss
(illustration)

Cheddar
(illustration)

Mozzarella
(illustration)

◎ **New Definition**   Cheese is a dairy product that can be soft, stringy, rubbery, or hard and can be called Cheddar, Swiss, Mozzarella, Longhorn, and Colby. It gives us protein and fat.

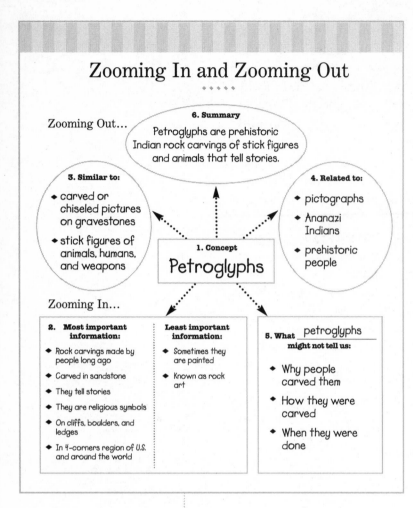

Zooming In and Zooming Out

• • • • •

Zooming Out...

6. Summary
Petroglyphs are prehistoric Indian rock carvings of stick figures and animals that tell stories.

3. Similar to:
◆ carved or chiseled pictures on gravestones
◆ stick figures of animals, humans, and weapons

4. Related to:
◆ pictographs
◆ Ananazi Indians
◆ prehistoric people

1. Concept
Petroglyphs

Zooming In...

2. Most important information:
◆ Rock carvings made by people long ago
◆ Carved in sandstone
◆ They tell stories
◆ They are religious symbols
◆ On cliffs, boulders, and ledges
◆ In 4-corners region of U.S. and around the world

Least important information:
◆ Sometimes they are painted
◆ Known as rock art

5. What petroglyphs **might not tell us:**
◆ Why people carved them
◆ How they were carved
◆ When they were done

A seventh grader created this Zooming In and Zooming Out organizer.

Internet Connection

www.randomhouse. com/wotd

This is the official site of "The Mavens' Word of the Day." It offers a new word or phrase and its definition each day, as well as links to pages with interesting information about language and the dictionary.

◎ **Zooming In and Zooming Out** is a strategy for teaching content-area vocabulary that blends word learning with concept development in grades 4 to 8 (Harmon & Hedrick, 2000). "Zooming" provides a close examination, "microscopic look," at a word or concept and a "panoramic view." (See sample left.) Use the strategy before reading to activate students' prior knowledge. Use it during reading to help students rely on context for meaning. And use it after reading to support students' interactions with text and one another as they review and reread. (See Appendix, page 121.)

Creating a "Zoom" organizer as a class can be a powerful experience. Your students will share ideas and use critical thinking to arrive at "close-up" views of the word (i.e., most and least important information related to word) and "big picture" views (i.e., similarities and relationships to the word). They brainstorm, read, and discuss to form a summary statement. Use the "Zoom" strategy sparingly, perhaps only for one or two words that represent the most critical concepts in a unit. Post completed organizers for students to use as a reference in class discussions and writing.

◎ **English Language Factoids** Carl Sandburg said "The English language hasn't got where it is by being pure." So teach students that English is made up of a smorgasbord of words from around the world. It is larger than many other languages and, as a result, enables us to describe a range of things, ideas, and experiences with great precision. And it is widely used around the world; if you don't know the language of the country you're visiting, it is usually not difficult to find someone who speaks English.

Share with students the following factoids (Lederer, 1991), as well as any others you may gather about English, to help them appreciate and understand our language and the importance of having a large vocabulary:

Factoids About the English Language

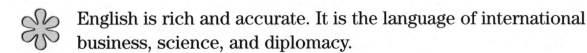

❋ English is rich and accurate. It is the language of international business, science, and diplomacy.

❋ 350 million people speak English exclusively and it is the second language of just as many people. Someone in nearly every country in the world speaks it.

❋ English is a huge and unique collection of more than 600,000 words. German is one-third as large and French is one-sixth this size.

❋ Three-quarters of the words in the dictionary are of foreign origin and many are pronounced the same in both languages, for example "camel"—Hebrew, "zoo"—Greek, "shampoo"—Hindi, "opera"—Italian.

❋ Half the books published in the world today are in English.

❋ English grows and changes daily. New terms from science, technology, other countries, and youth culture are regularly added to our dictionaries.

❋ The rules of English are simple, orderly, and consistent compared to other languages. For example, *fl-*, *sl-*, and *str-* and *-ame, -ipe,* and *-ot* consistently represent the same sounds. When *fl-ame, sl-ot* and *str-ipe* are put together, they are consistently pronounced the same.

Internet Connection

www.tprstorytelling.
com/story.htm

This site offers the
rationale, description,
sample lessons, and
references for TPRS.

◎ **TPRS: Total Physical Response Storytelling** (especially good for verbal/linguistic, interpersonal and bodily/kinesthetic learning) is a unique approach for teaching a foreign language to English speakers using all four cueing systems of language (Ray & Seely, 1997). You can use it to teach English to ESL learners, as well. Students acquire and practice vocabulary using a variety of communication skills: listening, speaking, reading, writing, gesturing, acting, and storytelling. Ellen Spruce, a middle-school foreign language teacher, uses TPRS to teach French to her English-speaking students, using a series of lessons that occur over a span of several days:

◆ **Teach a short list of words.** Present each word with an action or gesture that connects to the meaning of the word. For example, to teach the word for *eat*, Ellen says, *mange*, and represents it by putting an imaginary spoon to her mouth repeatedly. Then she acts out eating pieces of plastic fruit, saying *mange* and the French name for the fruit.

◆ **Have students produce and practice words in pairs.** Ellen pairs students, and has them read and perform words from a list. One student reads a target word and the other acts it out. They continue acting out words from the list, alternating roles.

◆ **Present a mini-story and have students retell it.** Ellen tells a three- to five-minute story she has written that includes the target vocabulary of five to six words students have just practiced. As she reads, she pauses at those words to let students act them out. Occasionally, she makes intentional mistakes and lets students correct her. She also asks short-answer and open-ended questions related to story content that students respond to. Then students retell the story to a partner.

◆ **Present a main story for students to retell and revise.** Once Ellen has written and read several mini-stories, she creates a main story using all the vocabulary from the mini-stories. This story may be two or three times as long as one mini-story and contain 15 to 20 new words. As Ellen reads the story, students take turns acting it out, using their own words to embellish and personalize it.

◆ **Encourage students to use new and old vocabulary to create original stories.** Students write their own stories, read them aloud, and pick classmates to act them out. In class and as homework, Ellen also has students create cartoon stories with captions using the list of target vocabulary, and asks them to write brief narratives to accompany their cartoons. (See sample on next page.)

TPRS includes a physical response to words and a critical vehicle—storytelling—that lets students use and expand acquired vocabulary by contextualizing it in high-interest stories they can hear, see, act out, retell, revise, and write. As Ellen's students add humor, creativity, and originality to their own versions of stories, they learn new words naturally. Ellen finds that her sixth graders take ownership of learning new words with TPRS and are highly motivated to communicate stories to their peers.

A TPRS cartoon with captions containing target vocabulary.

◎ **3-D Words** (especially good for visual, auditory, kinesthetic and tactile learning) is a strategy that builds vocabulary by requiring students to use the senses to attach meanings to words (Zivkovich, 1997). You can use it as a creative homework assignment to promote learning of technical vocabulary in science or social studies. Here is how it works:

◆ On Friday, each student selects a word to learn. You can also provide a list from which students can choose their words.

◆ As weekend homework, each student creates a 3-D collage of his or her word on an $8\frac{1}{2}$ x 11" piece of heavy paper, with definition and sample sentence. For example, one student chose the word *identical* and made his collage from sets of real objects such as two LifeSavers® and two paper clips. (See sample left.)

◆ On Monday, students present their collages to the class and post their 3-D Words on a word wall. During the week, everyone records the new words with definitions, sentences, and drawings in their vocabulary notebooks. You can also have a few students share their collages with the class over several days.

A sixth grader depicts "identical" as a 3-D Word.

◎ **I Have…Who Has?** (especially good for verbal/linguistic, interpersonal bodily/kinesthetic, and existential learning) uses listening and reading to reinforce the semantic cueing system and word meanings. Kristin Troeger introduced it to her fourth graders when she noticed many of them having trouble with difficult science vocabulary. She identifies 22 vocabulary words, one for each student in her class. On 3 x 5" cards, she writes a vocabulary word on one side and the definition of a *different* word on the other side. Each student gets a card and reads it silently before the game begins.

Then one student reads his word, saying "I have (vocabulary word)…" Then, he turns the card over, asks "Who has…?," and reads the definition. The student who has the word that fits the definition says "I have (vocabulary word)…" Then, she turns the card over, asks "Who has…?," and reads the definition. The game continues until everyone has had a turn.

Kristin's students love this game so much, they beg to play it every week, Over time, she has let them choose the words and make the cards themselves, requiring them to use textbooks, glossaries, and dictionaries to make sure definitions were correct. She checks the cards before the game starts. "I Have…Who Has…?" can also be played in smaller groups by giving each student several cards.

⊚ **Interview a Word** (especially good for verbal/linguistic, interpersonal, naturalistic, and existential learning) requires students to "become" a word and answer a series of questions asked by an interviewer. This strategy builds semantic and pragmatic knowledge of words.

First, select key words important to understanding a story or concept. Then, divide your class into teams and give each team a word and a list of questions about the word. Have students "become" the word and answer the questions. (See samples below, and Appendix, page 122, for a blank template.) The interviewer, either you or a student, asks team members each question, and they respond with the answers they've prepared, while the rest of class listens to the "interview." Then the class tries to guess the word.

Interview a Word
Prose

1 Who are your relatives?
Stories, writing, speech

2 Would you ever hurt anyone? Who? Why?
Yes, harsh words can be spoken or written about another person.

3 Are you useful? What is your purpose?
Yes, I keep traditions alive through storytelling and by keeping written stories.

4 What don't you like? Why?
I don't like people who use me to be cruel.

5 What do you love? Why?
I love to be spoken or written with correct grammar.

6 What are your dreams?
I dream of being used only to make people happy through good stories.

Interview a Word
Rejected

1 Who are your relatives?
My relatives are refused and snubbed.

2 Would you ever hurt anyone? Who? Why?
Yes, I would hurt someone who is talking to me because if I was talking to me and turn around I would hurt their feelings.

3 Are you useful? What is your purpose?
Yes, I'm useful because if someone asked you to do drugs I would reject them and walk away.

4 What don't you like? Why?
I don't like things that are bad accepted from people, because I'm forgotten about.

5 What do you love? Why?
I love it when people reject other people for bad things, because bad things are bad.

6 What are your dreams?
My dreams are for people to reject people because of drugs every time.

Interview a Word sheets for "prose" and "rejected"

Christin Messina's fifth graders love Interview a Word because it's a different way to learn. She loves it because "students must take on the role of that word and see a word from various perspectives." First, Christin explains and models the strategy by sharing a completed "Interview a Word" sheet for the term *prose* on an overhead transparency with her students. Then she divides the class into groups of four and gives each group a word. From Section 6 of *Dear Mr. Henshaw* by Beverly Cleary (William Morrow), about a boy who moves and goes to a new school, she chose *imitate, rejected, snoop,* and *disconnect,* all words she thought students needed to understand so they could relate to the main character, Leigh Botts.

Christin gives each group a blank interview sheet (see Appendix, page 122) and 10 minutes to talk and answer the questions before their interview. When she "interviews" each group, they read their responses (see samples, page 47) and the class tries to guess the word. When students have a hard time guessing the word, Christin has them review the chapter to find it. This part of the strategy is an excellent way to promote rereading, skimming, and scanning for specific information, and using a thesaurus or dictionary.

Christin's students enjoy "getting into" word meanings this way and so she has made the strategy a regular weekly occurrence. She says her students love the challenge of exploring words and their use through the interview format. They often add a dramatic voice to their interviews and she encourages impromptu ad-libs because she discovered that, often, students who aren't being interviewed have appropriate and interesting associations to share.

◎ **TNT** (especially good for verbal/linguistic, bodily/kinesthetic, and interpersonal learning) is a strategy Jodi Van Gaasback uses with her third graders after reading to reinforce word recognition and meaning. She selects words she feels students probably don't know but are key to their understanding a reading selection. Or she has students choose words from the story that they want to remember and use in their writing. Regardless of who chooses the words, though, she pre-teaches word meanings and pronunciations, making sure to use words in contexts students will understand. Then, she divides the class into groups of four or five students. She has each member of a group choose three words and write them on separate Popsicle® sticks or strips of tag board. She writes the word "BAM!" on ten sticks or strips and puts all the sticks or strips, word-end down, in a can labeled with the story title.

To play the game, each group sits in a circle and passes the can around. One by one, students choose a stick or strip and if the student chooses a vocabulary word, he reads the word, uses it in a sentence (asking a classmate for help if he gets stuck), and keeps the stick or strip. If a someone picks "BAM!" he must return all his words to the container,

and the game continues around the circle until no vocabulary words are left, or as long as time permits. The one with the most words at the end of the game is the winner—but Jodi says her students play with enthusiasm whether or not a winner is announced.

Jodi's students also enjoy playing TNT in pairs or threes. She has a collection of TNT cans with lids that hold words from various stories the class has read, and she encourages students to take it home to play TNT with parents and siblings for additional reinforcement.

S U M M A R Y

This chapter has provided you with basic information about vocabulary acquisition, identified common pitfalls to avoid, and given you general guidelines and ideas for enhancing your word-study program to reach every kind of learner. In the following chapters, I will introduce you to other teachers who use novel approaches to help their students learn new words by using context, word structure, word origins, and the Internet.

Using Context to Learn Words

◆ **G**ARTH WILLIAMS, illustrator of *Charlotte's Web* (White, Harper & Row), knows the power of a picture to communicate meaning. In one illustration, Wilbur, the downhearted pig who sees little of value in himself, finds the word *terrific* woven into his spider friend's web. When eight-year-old Tori talks about the text accompanying that illustration, and draws her own version of Wilbur smiling contentedly under the web, it's proof that she understands how the word terrific makes Wilbur feel. (See drawing below.) She may connect terrific to his wonderful friendship with Charlotte or to sympathetic Fern and her kind parents, Mr. and Mrs. Arable, since all of these characters make Wilbur feel terrific for different reasons. For Tori herself, terrific can hold a host of other associations, as well. She may connect it to how she felt after her last birthday party or during a hot afternoon of running through a lawn sprinkler with her best friend. Terrific may also remind her of what her father says when her brother pitches a "no-hitter." All of these situations enrich Tori's understanding of the word. For her and students like her, word meaning can emerge from context and context can give a word richer meanings.

Pictures provide a context that helps students identify and learn new words. ▶

Making Meaning With Context

Using context means weaving together information from several sources to unlock the meaning of an unknown word—sources such as pictures, words, and sentences occurring before and after the word, and the situation in which the reading occurs. Reading a variety of books and other print materials and using these information sources are probably the best ways to increase our vocabularies.

Schema, our organized prior knowledge and experience, plays an important role in using context successfully. Constance Weaver (1994) says we use schema to help us identify, and sometimes misidentify, unknown words and the context in which they appear. The success of a student's use of context depends on how much and what type of prior knowledge and background experiences she possesses. If she applies a rich fund of information, experiences, and language knowledge to the context surrounding an unknown word, her chances of determining its meaning increase. And, conversely, if she possesses little or no schema, she has only a small chance of using context successfully.

Let's look more closely at what makes up context:

◎ **Pictures** Graphic images in a selection, like Williams's drawings of the Arable family and the barnyard animals, are part of context. But pictures alone can't help a student determine the meaning of a word. He or she must have experiences or concepts to attach to those pictures to understand what they show and imply. Therefore, it's important to seize every opportunity to build students' schemas and teach them to use pictures to help identify words and determine their meanings. Later, I suggest ways to do this.

◎ **Context Within Text** The sentence and paragraph in which the unknown word appears also make up context. Their words help us to decide an unknown word's meaning. For example, words in this sentence from *Charlotte's Web* may have helped Tori define *terrific*: "Wilbur, who really felt terrific, stood quietly swelling out his chest and swinging his snout from side to side." Tori may connect "swelling out his chest" with being happy or proud, as when she stands tall to lead her class in a song or when her brother accepts a trophy for his baseball team.

Grammar can also give Tori clues to the word. For example, in the phrase "Wilbur, who really felt terrific…," *felt* may prompt Tori to think about words that explain Wilbur's state of mind. And when she combines that grammar clue with what she knows about the grapho-phonemics, perhaps the initial consonant *t* and the *if* in the middle of the word, these sources may alert her to the meaning of the word.

Context also refers to clues from the entire text. Clues to *terrific*, for instance, may come from the larger context of things that make Wilbur feel terrific, such as the fact that his pen was always full of clean straw and the crate that Lurvy built for him, with the sign that read "Zuckerman's Famous Pig."

◎ **Context Beyond Text** Context also involves the situation or environment in which the reading occurs. Tori may use different strategies when she reads in school than she does when she reads at home, and may, therefore, interpret words differently in each context. At home, she may ask her mother to tell her a difficult word. At school, she may be prompted to use the Fix-Up Strategies described in Chapter 1, since that is what her teacher expects. Or she may interpret a word such as *permanent* differently if she reads it in a story while waiting for her mother in a beauty salon than if she reads it on a bag of concrete at a building site.

Good readers weave a variety of context clues together to help determine the meaning of an unknown word. When a student uses context with other strategies, she will most likely be successful in determining, remembering, and learning new words.

Context means weaving together different kinds of information—pictures, as well as information from within and beyond the text. ▶

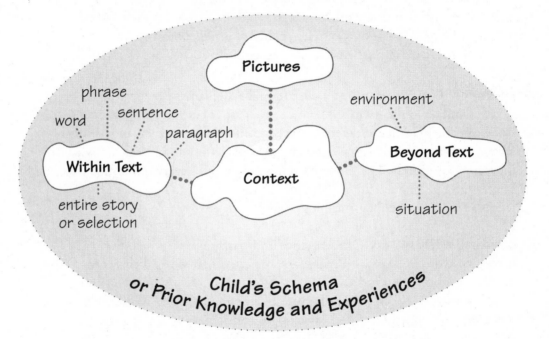

When Context Doesn't Help

Sometimes context doesn't hold enough clues to help us determine the meaning of an unknown word. Here are some reasons why:

◎ **Prior knowledge and experiences aren't broad enough.** When a student lacks schema to connect to unknown words, learning them can be difficult. But one who knows, for example, what *shrink* means because of what happened to her new shirt in the clothes drier may use this schema to understand the meaning of *shrinking* or *shrink* in a different context.

◎ **Pictures are inaccurate or unavailable.** Students who over-rely on pictures for meaning often find themselves at a dead end. This can happen for two reasons:

◆ Pictures aren't always accurate. To get help with the meaning of *auburn*, a student may look at a picture in the story. If the picture shows a girl with black hair, the child may conclude that *auburn* means *black*.

◆ Pictures aren't always available. As the reading level of books increases, the number of pictures decreases to accommodate more text. So when students begin to read longer, more difficult books with few pictures, this strategy fails them.

◎ **The sentence or paragraph doesn't contain helpful words.** Sometimes the passage in which the word appears doesn't give clues to its meaning. For example, in the passage below there are no synonyms, definitions, antonyms, or adjectives to give clues to the meaning of the words *worsening*, *alcoholism*, and *medical*. Clues may appear elsewhere in the piece, but in these brief excerpts, context doesn't help.

About Russia

Russia, the world's largest country, stretches across 11 time zones and has a **territory** of 6.8 million square miles. It has 89 **provinces**. As of the beginning of the year 2000, Russia had a **population** of 145.5 million people. Russia's population has been **shrinking** since the 1991 Soviet collapse, mainly because of **worsening** economic conditions, widespread **alcoholism**, a low birth rate and bad **medical** care.

◆ **territory:** "6.8 million square miles" gives clues to meaning
◆ **provinces:** knowing the U.S. has 50 states can help with meaning
◆ **population:** "145.5 million people" gives clues to meaning
◆ **shrinking:** "a low birth rate" gives clues to meaning
◆ **worsening:** the text doesn't help
◆ **alcoholism:** the text doesn't help
◆ **medical:** the text doesn't help

When context is unreliable, therefore, and doesn't help students decipher new words, you may want to pre-teach some vocabulary and focus on vocabulary-building activities such as Zooming In and Zooming Out and the Concept Definition Map from Chapter 2, or strategies presented in other chapters.

Using Context Effectively

Pictures and words within text, as well as the situation or environment beyond the text, often help students draw from their schemas to learn new words. Here are some ways to help students in grades 3 to 8 use context effectively, organized around the three information sources described earlier.

Pictures

The old saying "A picture is worth 1,000 words" is certainly true. Pictures are one of the first clues readers rely on. They often contain a lot of information students can use to unlock an unknown word's meaning and remember it. Here are some ideas for using pictures effectively:

◎ **Word Pictures** is a strategy Amy Litchfield uses with third graders to reinforce words related to units of study. It's fun because students connect words to pictures they draw. (See sample below.) Here's what to do:

- ◆ Choose, or have students choose, a vocabulary word to draw.

- ◆ Tell students to draw a simple picture of the word.

- ◆ Have them fill in the picture by printing the word inside the object. Use colored pens or pencils to make words stand out.

- ◆ Depending on age and ability, have students add details and pictures of other related words to the picture, such as *seaweed*.

- ◆ Share and display Word Pictures in the classroom so students can learn new words from one another.

- ◆ Assign words as homework or for extra credit.

This strategy works best with words that can easily be represented in pictures. Therefore, nouns are good choices, but verbs, adjectives, and adverbs can also work. Amy knows this strategy shouldn't be the sole method of teaching or practicing vocabulary. If it's overused, she says, "it can quickly become a tiresome task!" But it can be a motivating vocabulary strategy that uses the context of pictures to reinforce learning.

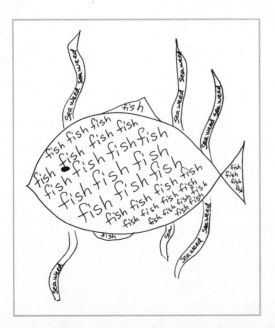

◀ *A student's Word Picture for "fish."*

Joyce Lewis uses a similar strategy to help her eighth graders learn science vocabulary. As a starting point for learning how to use a microscope, she wanted them to know the names of each part. So she had them "build" a microscope with words. Joyce reviewed the parts of a microscope with the class, using a poster and sticky notes. Then she had her students draw their own microscopes by drawing "word pictures" for each part. This helped students used the specialized vocabulary of microscopes, as they worked with them.

A sixth grader's Word Picture for "microscope." ▶

◎ **Key Symbols** is an idea Paul Walenesky uses to help his students learn new words. Paul feels it's important to teach the power of symbols and their ability to convey meaning. "Symbols stick in our minds," he says. "They can bridge to verbal text messages. They activate our visual intelligence and they are an enduring recall tool." His fifth graders study magazines, newspapers, television, and the Internet for examples of how companies use symbols to attract attention and convey meaning in advertisements.

They also create their own symbols, since Paul finds that students learn new words more easily when they draw and write about them. For example, to help his students learn about *heat* and *matter*, Paul had them draw the picture next to the word and then make notes of related and important information. (See sample next page.)

Similarly, to pre-teach important social studies vocabulary, Paul created a key symbol for words associated with westward expansion in the United States. Students wrote these vocabulary words, drew the symbols for them in their learning logs, and referred to them during the unit. Paul says, "Drawing a key symbol for a word first is often enough to prompt my students to research and write more than they normally would about that word." (See sample next page.)

These picture-based strategies, and others you will read about later, not only help students learn technical vocabulary in science, social studies, and math, but also enhance their graphic representation skills and their interest in drawing. Of course, providing the right supplies for these

Heat   Matter

- Most of our heat comes from the radiation of the sun.

- A measurement of the heat of reaction can be made with an instrument called an calorimeter.

- conduction is a point-by-point process of heat transfer.

- Another method of transfering heat energy from one place to another is called radiation.

- Benjamin Thompson revived the kinetic theory of heat

- The six main sources of heat are: Sun, Fire, Earth, Chemical Reaction, Friction and Nuclear Energy.

- electrons can connect to form molecules

- Matter appears to be static or motionless, but actualy moving.

- During one single second, each gas molecule has about 5000 million collision with other molecules.

- Billions of collisions keep a balloon in the air.

Key Symbols help students learn new words for a science and social studies unit.

---

strategies—colored pencils and markers, colored paper, and so forth—is a good motivator.

Like pictures, other kinds of graphics, too, provide context. The size, style, and weight of type; the use of color; and the illustrator's style can all serve to make words easier to identify, learn, and remember. Diagrams, charts, and captions also give young readers a helpful context in much the same way pictures do. In fact, sometimes students who can't read a difficult text can easily understand a new word or concept by looking at a graphic organizer or reading a caption and studying the picture to which it refers. So don't overlook these aspects of print.

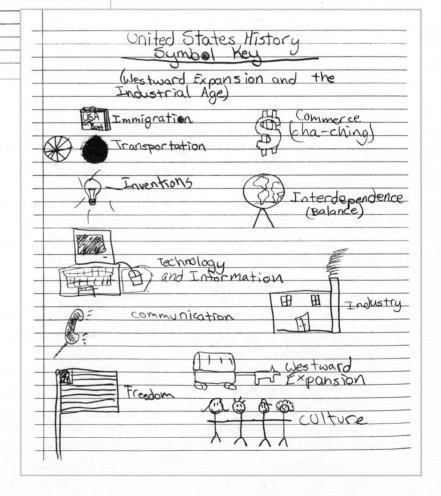

United States History
Symbol Key

(Westward Expansion and the Industrial Age)

Immigration   Commerce (cha-ching)

Transportation

Inventions   Interdependence (Balance)

Technology and Information

Industry

communication

Freedom   Westward Expansion

Culture

Context Within Text

Clues within a sentence, paragraph, or whole text can lead students to a word's meaning. So it's important to nudge readers to "keep reading" when they get stuck. By reading beyond the unknown word, students often find clues to a word's meaning long after the word's appearance in the text.

Here's an example: A student may not recognize words like *whomped, trounced, routed,* or *skunked* in isolation, but when he reads them in headlines in the newspaper's sports section, he's more likely to guess that the words are synonyms for *beat*. He may also realize the words are verbs because they end in "ed."

Words that come before and after an unknown word, such as synonyms, antonyms, adjectives and definitions, are often helpful clues. Read the paragraph entitled "About Russia" on page 53 and see if you can infer the meaning of *territory* from the context. The adjective "largest" and synonym "country" probably help you define *territory* as a landmass of some sort. The phrase "square miles," which follows *territory*, describes land size and, therefore, provides another clue to the meaning of *territory*. You can infer the meaning of *population* from the phrase "145.5 million people." You may infer the meaning of *shrinking* from the word *low*. But the paragraph's context does not give clues to the words *worsening, alcoholism,* or *medical*. For these words you might need to use the dictionary. Here are several strategies for using context within a sentence, paragraph, or whole text:

◎ **Excerpt Errors** is an idea Nichole Purdy uses to combine spelling, social studies, and vocabulary development. Students rely on the context of a sentence or paragraph, and their knowledge of the topic, to correct errors and learn new words.

On Monday, Nichole gives her fifth graders a vocabulary/spelling list containing words related to the unit they are studying in social studies, for example *colonists, patriots, minutemen, Tories, Hessians, George Washington, King George, smugglers, boycott,* and *blockade*. The words come from their social studies textbook and a related novel that students are reading in language arts, such as *The Fighting Ground* by Avi (HarperCollins).

Each morning for the rest of the week, students come into the room to find an excerpt from their social studies text or the novel written on the chalkboard. The excerpt might contain blank spaces to fill in or intentional spelling errors or misinformation to correct. For example, of the six errors in the excerpt from *The Fighting Ground* on the next page, three of them involve target vocabulary or spelling words. Together, the class finds the errors, and then individual students come to the board to correct them. Students write the correct sentence in their journal.

Internet Connection

www.eduplace. com/tales/

This site is for grades 3 and up. Kids supply 10 to 15 words, and the program creates a story using them. Students must supply words for various parts of speech (for example, *a plural noun*, *a large number*, *an adjective*, *a male friend*). The site also publishes kids' own Wacky Web Tales.

"When the patreots dressed up like American Indians and threw the coffee into New York Harbor, _____ got angry and sent ships to _____ the harbor."

corrected version:

"When the patriots dressed up like American Indians and threw the tea into Boston Harbor, King George got angry and sent ships to blockade the harbor."

Context helps students correct errors in a text excerpt.

On Friday afternoon, students take a two-part test that Nichole "split grades." In part one, she gives students a definition or sentence with a blank, and they must fill in the correct term. Part two is a typical spelling test—Nichole says the word in a sentence and has students write it down. She gives separate grades for social studies (for which she accepts incorrect spelling) and for spelling. That way, she can assess students' content vocabulary and spelling knowledge individually.

Clue Words is a strategy Michelle Herceg uses to pre-teach vocabulary to fourth graders. It helps them learn to use context within text to figure out and remember difficult words. Here is what Michelle suggests:

- Review a story you're planning to share with students, and choose four or five new words they will need to comprehend the story.

- Write a short paragraph on chart paper or a transparency containing the new words. Be sure to underline the words and include context clues to help show each word's meaning. (See Michelle's example below.)

The potato <u>harvest</u> is a very busy time of year on the farm. There are many things to do to prepare for it. One thing we need to do is <u>irrigate</u> the land in order for the potatoes to grow. Then we have to pick 7 <u>bushels</u> of potatoes. We work long hours everyday! I see the sun come up in the morning and watch it disappear below the <u>horizon</u> every day. When I come in for dinner, I am <u>famished</u>. After dinner I do my chores. I wash the dishes, clean my room, and <u>churn</u> the butter for one hour with a wooden spoon. When I finish with my chores, my mom <u>insists</u> I go right to bed so I will be ready for another busy day on the farm.

- Read the paragraph to students and then think aloud about how you use context to figure out the first word's meaning. Circle the "clue words" that help.

- Ask students to think aloud and circle the clue words for the rest of the underlined words.

- Have students come up with definitions for the new words, based on what they learned from context.

When they've figure out the definitions of all the words, Michelle's students sometimes write a short paragraph using a few of them. (See sample right.) This lets Michelle see if they understand the new vocabulary. She says, "When my students begin to use these words in their own writing and everyday language, I attribute it to directly teaching new words in context. I think this is a very useful way to build larger vocabularies."

> As I churned the butter I watched the sun go below the horizon. From smelling the food cooking on the stove I was famished. But I still had to irrigate the crops. It is harvesting time and I've been very busy latly. Well my parents insisted I should have helped. We've been picking bushels and bushels of different crops. It's very tiring. Well dinner is almost ready. I can't wait to eat.

Venessa uses new words in a paragraph.

Here are some variations on Clue Words:

- After thinking aloud and circling clue words as a class, have students work in pairs to figure out the meaning of new words. Then ask them to share their definitions with the class.

- Ask students to write down their definitions and compare them to the dictionary's. They will quickly learn that most words have more than one meaning.

- Have each student write sentences or a paragraph containing at least three new words. Divide students into pairs and have them read their work to each other.

- Put students in charge. Ask two students to work together to survey the story, pick out words they see as potentially difficult for their classmates, and create a paragraph that gives context clues to word meanings. Then have them teach the class how to use context to arrive at the meaning of these new words.

Guessed Meanings combines prediction and context to help students learn new words (Poindexter, 1994). Here is how it works:

- ◆ Choose a text you plan to read aloud and, from it, identify a few words that students may have trouble understanding.

- ◆ List the words in a four-column chart. (See sample below.) These words are from the first 20 pages of *Pedro's Journal* by Pam Conrad (Scholastic), the log belonging to a cabin boy who accompanied Christopher Columbus to the New World.

- ◆ Invite students to guess the meanings of all the words and write their definitions in the second column.

- ◆ Begin reading the text. As you read, have students note when they hear a targeted word.

- ◆ Reread the sentence and paragraph in which the word appears and have students "test" their definitions to see if they make sense.

- ◆ If they don't make sense, have students revise their definitions, based on the context, and write them in the third column.

- ◆ Give students the dictionary definitions to add to the fourth column. Once students are familiar with this strategy, you might share dictionary definitions for only those words they couldn't guess.

Guessed Meanings require students to look at context and the dictionary for word meanings.

Over time, students learn that the more they rely on context to make predictions, the less they need to use the dictionary. You can reinforce this by consistently noting how their initial definitions evolve to contextual definitions and finally to dictionary definitions.

You can also have students read a selection silently. Then, in pairs or small groups, they can choose words and carry out the activity, using a four-column worksheet. (See Appendix, page 123, for a blank template.) Once students are familiar with the strategy, let them work independently to identify new or difficult words and fill in the sheet.

Guessed Meanings

· · · · ·

Word	Guessed Meaning	Context Meaning	Dictionary Meaning
Roster	list line	list of people on a ship	list or role of personnel
Mandarins	little oranges collars on shirts plants	important people princes, kings	a high Chinese official
Careening	tipping speeding	toppling	leaning sideways tilt or tip
Caulkers	workers carpenters boaters	workers carpenters	workers who make wood watertight
Maravedis	marauders thieves bank robbers pirates	coins money	Spanish coins
Forebodes	whispers tells	portends suggests	predicts foretells

◎ **Guess and Check** is a strategy that requires students to use context and word structure to arrive at a new word's meaning (Vazquez, 1995). Kristie D'Addezio uses it successfully with fifth graders. Using the template in the Appendix, page 124, follow these steps:

◆ Give students a copy of the Guess and Check template with a list of new words from the story or textbook selection you're planning to have them read.

◆ Have them write the new words under "Unknown Word."

◆ As they read the text independently, have them use different strategies, such as searching for context clues and looking for prefixes, suffixes, and root words, to fill in "Clues" and "Guess" columns.

◆ Have students use the dictionary, thesaurus, encyclopedia, or a glossary to check their guesses, and write the published definition under "Check." (See sample below.)

◆ Encourage students to add other unfamiliar words from the text to their charts.

"Guess and Check" differs from "Guessed Meanings" in that students search for clues and guess *as* they read. For "Guessed Meanings," students make guesses *before* reading, based on background knowledge, not on context or word structure.

Guess and Check requires students to find clues, guess word meaning, and check references for accuracy. ▷

Guess and Check

· · · · ·

Unknown Word	Clues	Guess	Check
Coaxing p. 11	placed	to convince	to persuade or try to persuade
Gait p. 18	clumsy	the way they walk	the way of moving a foot

◎ **Reciprocal Teaching** is a strategy that helps struggling readers of all ages rely on context clues and each other to learn new words (Palinscar & Brown, 1988). After modeling the procedure, reading specialist Sue Biddle has a student leader guide a group discussion, emphasizing four comprehension strategies:

◈ **Question** each other about the story.

◈ **Summarize** the text.

◈ **Clarify** the meaning of the story and any hard words.

◈ **Predict** what will happen next in the story.

Sue says that the *Question* and *Clarify* steps are most important for word learning, as students identify words or phrases they don't understand and other group members help by giving their definitions. Here's an example of Reciprocal Teaching in action, based on a section of *Out of the Dust* by Karen Hesse (Scholastic) called "Devoured," about a young girl who lived in the Oklahoma Dust Bowl during the Depression.

James, student leader:	"I have two QUESTIONS and I need CLARIFICATION. What does it mean "…whirred like a thousand engines"? And what does the word *tassels* mean?"
Amanda:	"I can CLARIFY. When grasshoppers fly, their wings move so fast they make a whirring noise and maybe it sounded like a lawn mower engine. And, *tassels* are on corn. They're the yellow stuff on the tops that means it's getting ready to eat."
Todd:	"Also, I can CLARIFY. It says the grasshoppers came in a big "cloud," so it must have sounded like a lot of lawn mower engines or motorcycles even."
Raisha:	"Also, I'll CLARIFY. "Apple cores" is another clue that tells us it's summer or fall. And, that's when corn gets its *tassels*."

Students base their explanations of new words on context clues by identifying words, phrases, or ideas from the passage that help to infer the meaning. Sue says this helps students monitor their own vocabulary development. They are more willing to ask for clarification when it is part of the four-step comprehension process.

Laurie Whitney uses Reciprocal Teaching regularly with fifth graders. She gives students sticky notes and encourages them to jot down their questions about their reading, and any words they don't understand. Students use these notes to guide their post-reading discussion. Laurie says that when that first student asks for clarification of a hard word, it makes everyone feel comfortable. The number of clarifications increases, and so does word learning.

Reciprocal Teaching actively involves students in monitoring their own comprehension and controlling the story discussion. Most important, students learn how to learn new words independently.

◎ **Word Hunt** is a strategy Doris Brosnan uses to help her students revise their writing. In Word Hunt, students use the context of their own stories to find more accurate and original words to replace "worn-out" ones, such as *nice*, *good*, *sad*, and *big*. For this strategy, Doris has several copies available of *A First Thesaurus* (Wittels & Greisman, Golden Books), which contains over 2,000 words with synonyms and antonyms.

Doris's third-grade students are writing individual animal storybooks for the classroom library. Her goal is to help students improve their clarity of ideas and grab readers' attention with accurate, descriptive words. One student, Laura, is working on a story about a puppy that is banished from its home for reckless behavior. Thomas is writing about a walrus that is captured and taken from its iceberg home by a TV crew. Both of the students' drafts contain a sentence describing the main character as "sad."

Doris introduces Word Hunt to Laura and Thomas in a writers' conference, by asking if there is a more interesting word to use instead of *sad*. Laura can't think of one on her own. So, Doris suggests checking their thesaurus. They open to the appropriate page, noting the strings of words attached to each entry. Together, they count 12 words for *sad*. No definitions are offered, only individual synonyms in black and one antonym in red, so it's hard to distinguish which one is the best choice.

As she reads the thesaurus's words with Laura and Thomas, Doris describes their differences. They all know what *unhappy* means, but that word is so close to *sad* that they decide it's not right. She tells the students that *depressed* means sadness that lasts a long time, and sometimes the person does not even know what he is depressed about. Thomas tells her right away that *depressed* is not the word he needs since the walrus has just been taken, and he knows who did it! She tells the children that *blue* conveys a mild sadness, less than *depressed*, that also lingers. They reject *blue*.

At this point, Laura and Thomas are excited, having all these sophisticated choices available to them. They truly are on a Word Hunt. They watch Doris consult a dictionary for *downhearted* and connect the meaning with her own experiences—that feeling of being beaten by what has happened. Thomas considers that word because his walrus is in a cage and cannot see a way of escape. As Doris probes, Thomas tells her that the walrus wants to get back to his mother. He decides that *downhearted* is the perfect word.

Downhearted also strikes a chord with Laura, as she latches onto the idea of "someone not knowing if there is any help or hope." She writes it in her sentence. She tries *dejected* as well, since her pup, Derby, feels like he does not have a friend in the world.

Doris believes that, before they go on a Word Hunt, students should know the purpose of finding the right word. "They learn how to make choices as they observe my modeling a word hunt, using sources, thinking through the connotations, selecting the best word, and embedding it in a sentence to show its meaning. Later on, I smile when I see these children examining the reference books on their own and I see that a wondrous journey with words has begun for them!"

◎ **Super Word Web** is a strategy that "uses a visual organizer to develop depth and dimension of word knowledge" (Johnson & Rasmussen, 1998). It can be used as a post-reading activity to help students use context to enrich their word knowledge, or as a pre-reading activity to promote comprehension of a key word or concept. This strategy is particularly effective for upper-grade students. Teach it this way:

◆ Introduce the target word, such as *pandemonium*, by presenting it to students in a sentence that gives clues to its meaning.

◆ Give the word's definition from the dictionary, a glossary, or context, for example, "a place or scene of chaos, noise, or confusion."

◆ On a chart, write the word above a box large enough to hold several other words. (See sample below.)

◆ Provide three or four synonyms for the word (from the dictionary, glossary, or context) and write them in the box, for example *chaos, mayhem, bedlam*.

◆ List or draw three or four images you associate with the synonyms and write them around the box. Connect these words to the box with lines.

◆ Have students copy these webs into their vocabulary notebooks or display them in the classroom so they can refer to them while reading, writing, and talking.

After you have modeled this strategy, assign pairs of students different words and have them work together to complete a Super Word Web. Then, have students present their webs and share the process they used to create them. (See Appendix, page 125, for a blank template.)

Super Word Web
- - - - -

◎ **Sentence:** There was **pandemonium** at the soccer game and several people were trampled.

pandemonium
(word)

chaos	
mayhem	screaming voices
	running people
bedlam	being squashed
	being pushed and shoved

(synonyms)   (things that describe it)

a crowd roaring
(example)

◁ *A Super Word Web for "pandemonium."*

Context Beyond Text

Understanding the setting or situation in which reading occurs can give readers clues to the meaning of unknown words, too. Here's an example: When the word *invalid* appears on a sign at the Registry of Motor Vehicles, you may guess it means "no longer legal or valid" and pronounce it appropriately. But if the same word appears on a sign in your doctor's office, you may conclude that *invalid* means "a person who is bedridden." In both cases, the word's environment—its context—gives strong clues to its meaning and pronunciation. Here is a way to show your students how to use clues beyond text to figure out unknown words:

◎ **Think-Aloud** is a strategy to show students how you, as a more expert reader, figure out words you don't recognize by articulating your thought processes. It's important to draw from what you see in the text, as well as your understandings about words beyond the text. Here's what a think-aloud might look like, based on the paragraph entitled "About Russia" on page 53.

Teacher: "Here's an example of what I think when I don't know a word. I want to show you the process I use so you can try to do something like it when you meet a word you don't know. I don't recognize that 'R' word in the title of this boxed insert from the front page of the newspaper. Without reading it I can guess it's about national or international news because I know our paper puts local and regional news in an inside section. So, I can guess the word that begins with 'R' isn't going to be 'Rushville,' a small town nearby. And, I know it isn't going to be 'rushing' because it has a capital "R" and it has no 'ing' at the end. When I read the first line 'Russia, the world's largest country....' then I can guess the 'R' word better."

Here's another example:

Teacher: "I'm not sure I know the meaning of 'province.' But let's see, I know there are 50 states in the United States and this says '89 provinces.' So, I know what a state is and I'll just have to take a guess that a province is something like a state."

It's important to seize every opportunity to broaden and enrich students' schemas with explanations of new ideas and concepts, and "hands-on" experiences. Here are two ideas that will do just that, based on kinesthetic learning and classroom drama:

◎ **Jeopardy** is a game Lora McAvoy plays with her sixth graders to help them use what they already know to learn new words. First, identify several new multisyllabic words from the dictionary that contain a prefix, suffix, or root that students know—for example, *miscalculation*, *reminiscence, fixative, subcutaneous,* and *centripetal.* Put the list on the board, choose a word, and give students its definition. Students answer in the form of a question and explain how they arrived at their answer. Here are two examples of what Jeopardy looks like in action:

EXAMPLE #1

Teacher: The definition of this word is "below the skin."
Student: Is the word *subcutaneous*?
Teacher: Yes. How did you know that?
Student: I know that *sub* in *submarine* means *under* and a submarine goes under water.

EXAMPLE #2

Teacher: This word means "figuring something out incorrectly."
Student: Is the word *miscalculation*?
Teacher: Yes. How did you know?
Student: I remembered *mischief* is to do something that's bad and I know *calculate* means to figure something out.

Jeopardy taps into what students already know about words and promotes lively discussions about word derivations and structure. It is a game students of all ages and abilities enjoy. And, you can encourage students to use the dictionary, thesaurus, and glossary as they play it.

Word Theater is a strategy Bridget Vavra, a reading specialist, uses with struggling readers to help them learn words through improvisation and drama. Acting out a word's meaning lets students "live" the word and remember it. Choose key words from a story students have just read and write them on slips of paper. Put the slips in a container and have each student pick one to act out for the group. You may want to pair up shy students with a friend who can give them support and confidence.

One by one, Bridget's students:

- Write the word on the board and pronounce it.

- Use the word at least twice in the skit and show its meaning through actions. For example, students might pantomime a scene that gives clues to the meaning of *hoist,* such as raising a flag or lifting a heavy box from the floor to a high shelf.

- See if the audience has learned the word. The student may say, "Now, tell us what *hoist* means to you and use it in a new sentence."

Word Theater benefits both the "actor" and the audience. It requires the actor to process a word's meaning and translate it into movement and action. They must also write the word, say it, and listen to the audience define it. The audience sees the word written out, hears it pronounced, and learns from it being acted out.

◎ **Picture Dictionaries** are another way to encourage students to look beyond text to find meanings of new words. Kristin Passante's fifth graders make dictionaries for language arts, science, social studies, health, and math units. (See ideas for dictionary use in Chapter 5.) Together, Kristin and her students decide which words they need to know to understand the unit. She involves students in the decision making because they know better than anyone the words they need to learn. Kristin says, "Sometimes I am amazed at the words I take for granted that students know, when they really don't understand them."

The students look up the words in classroom dictionaries or textbook glossaries and write paraphrased definitions in their individual dictionaries. Then, because Kristin believes pictures are an important key to remembering words, she has students do drawings to represent each word, write a definition, and write a sentence containing the word. This is triple reinforcement for learning the words. (See samples below.)

Kristin Troeger takes Picture Dictionary one step further with her fourth-grade students. After finishing a book or a science or social studies unit, she assigns each student a word or lets them choose one they want to learn. First, students look their word up in the dictionary. Then, on a

Internet Connection

www.randomhouse.com/words/

This section of the Random House site has many fun activities that keep students up to date on "hot" new words. It also helps them see how slang and technical vocabulary regularly change our lexicon. Students can ask questions about a word and send their proposals for new words online.

gargantuan   gastropod

(gar·ri·son (gär/ĭsən) noun
A military post.

There used to be a garrison called Fort Duquesne.

discrimination   dishonor

disheveled. adj. (di shev/ld) not in neat order; mussed or rumpled; untidy.

When I woke up my hair was so disheveled.

Creating pages for a Picture Dictionary exposes students to guide words, diacritical marks, and pronunciations, as well as to word meanings.

sheet of paper, they write the two guide words that appear at the top right- and left-hand corners of the dictionary page where they found their word. Next, students write the word, its syllables, pronunciation, part of speech, and definition. Then, they draw a picture to represent the word and, at the bottom of the page, write the word in a sentence. Kristin often collates these dictionary pages into a class book or lets students make their own books.

This strategy not only enhances students' vocabulary skills, but referencing skills as well. For example, it exposes them to guide words, a tool that make using the telephone book, dictionary, thesaurus, and encyclopedia quicker and easier. It also exposes students to diacritical marks, pronunciations, and multiple meanings. Kristin says her students learn a lot about the target words and have fun in the process.

◎ **Lift-the-Flap Words** stretch students' schemas for words by requiring them to use context beyond the text. When her fourth-grade students finish reading a story or content selection, reading specialist Sue Biddle has each student choose four words they want to learn. They fold an $8\frac{1}{2}$ x 11" piece of paper in half lengthwise and make four equal flaps by cutting the folds. (See sample below.) On each flap they write one target word. Under each flap they add appropriate information about the word: its definition, a synonym, an antonym, a sentence that contains the word, and a picture that represents the word. The sentence must present the word in a way that is unrelated to the text from which it came, so that students demonstrate their understanding of it in a different context.

When all information is filled in for each word, students take turns in pairs or small groups reading a sentence, saying "blank" for the missing word, and calling on a partner to guess the word. This not only helps students attach meaning to new words, but also reinforces correct pronunciation.

Clearly, context is a powerful tool for word learning. But it is even more powerful it is if it is used along with other strategies. Doris Brosnan, a reading–language arts specialist, uses her poem "If You Find a New Word" with students of all

mountain

◆ a raised part of the earth's surface

◆ **synonym**— gigantic hill

◆ **antonym**—valley

....

The avalanche roared down the <u>mountain</u> and caught the skier.

plateau | valley | stream

ages and abilities to remind them to use all vocabulary strategies available to them.

Doris posts a chart-size version of the poem in her classroom and makes copies of it for each student to keep and use as a bookmark. When students run into difficulty with a new word, Doris helps them work their way through each step in the poem.

"If You Find a New Word"
by Doris Brosnan

♦ ♦ ♦ ♦ ♦

If you find a new word, here's a clue
To help you know what to do.

Go back to the new word's source.
Read the sentence again, of course.

Think about what it means.
Check that it is what it seems.

Take the word down to its base.
And know the phonics just in case
…you see those letters in another place.

Now, say the sentence in another way.
That's how the meaning of the word will stay!

♦ ♦ ♦ ♦

S U M M A R Y

Studies show mixed results in terms of how well students learn word meanings from context (Beck & McKeown, 1991; Rupley, Logan, & Nichols, 1999). Sometimes context is helpful, but often context does not contain enough clues to a word's meaning. Sometimes students know how to get clues from context and sometimes they don't. So, it is important to teach students how to use the different kinds of contexts discussed in this chapter, coupled with other strategies. In the next chapters, I share some of those strategies. You will learn ways of applying grammar, chunking or dividing words into component parts, examining root words for meaning, and using resources to boost word learning.

Using Structure to Learn Words

STUDENTS ACQUIRE WORDS when they are immersed in word-rich environments where they have opportunities to hear and use language. Reading, being read to, listening, speaking, and writing to communicate a message all build word knowledge. But it is also important to draw students' attention to word structure. Awareness of the way letters go together to make words not only helps students pronounce and spell words, but also gives them clues to their meaning.

In fact, to acquire vocabulary, it's helpful to many English learners and struggling readers to hear the structure of words. For example, fifth-grader Tyquan, who recently arrived here from Laos, is learning English as a second language. He will probably learn to read and write English more easily and quickly if he learns to speak it first. Hearing the sounds and structure of words, and saying words, will prepare him for reading and writing. For students with language delays and those who struggle with literacy, spoken language often is the scaffold for making meaning from print. And, when students can hear, speak, read, and write a word, it speeds their learning of that word.

Concepts About Words

What do students need to know about words to make learning them easier? According to Pinnell and Fountas (1998), there are several concepts about words that every reader should know. Tyquan and students like him need to know that a word means something, it is made up of letters, the letters go from left to right, there is white space on both sides of a word, and words go together to make a message.

When Tyquan hears a spoken word and says it, he can also look at the structure of the printed word and begin to understand that:

◎ A word has a special shape or configuration.

◎ Some words have patterns (for example, -ame, -ike, -ot).

◎ Most letters in a word stand for sounds but some are silent (for example, "ni<u>gh</u>t").

◎ Some words have "chunks" of letters (for example, "<u>un</u>-<u>happy</u>" and "<u>snow</u>-<u>man</u>").

◎ One word may help to unlock the meaning of another word (for example, "drama" and "dramatically").

Many students seem to understand and use this knowledge intuitively, while others need the concepts—along with opportunities for applying them—pointed out to them. For example, beginning readers and English learners often benefit from listening to taped stories as they follow the words in the book. As students match spoken words to printed words, they begin to understand the one-to-one correspondence between speech and print, and gain knowledge about words.

Reading and hearing stories is the best way to build students' awareness about words. But students also need other opportunities to see how words look in isolation to build their sight vocabulary, words they recognize and understand quickly without using context or letter sounds to figure them out. The next two ideas not only build vocabulary, but spelling skills as well. They are especially useful with new or struggling readers and English learners.

◎ **Box-It** is a way to help students become aware of a word's physical characteristics or configuration, by requiring them to outline the shape of it. The activity helps students learn the word as a unit, drawing their attention to the ascending and descending letters. As such, often longer words, such as *grandmother* and *elephant*, are easier to learn than shorter words, such as *than*, *then*, and *this*, because longer words have more distinctive shapes. (See sample next page.) Once students begin to notice those shapes, and recognize a fair number of words on sight, it's time to focus on letter sounds, clusters, and chunks. The best time to use Box-It is when you first teach a word, for example before reading a story or content selection, or when you introduce a new spelling list. You can draw boxes around a few sample words with the whole class, and then have students do it on their own with other words.

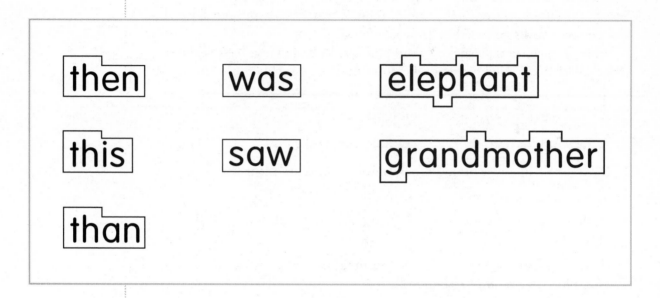

Box-It focuses attention on the shapes of words.

🌀 **Graph and Guess** trains the eye to "visualize" words. This is important because students often recognize and remember words by how they look. Place students in pairs. Working with a pre-determined list of words, one student chooses a word and colors in squares on a piece of graph paper for each letter of the word, using two squares above the baseline for ascending letters and two squares below for descending letters. Then, while referring to the list, the other student tries to guess the word and spells it as he points to each square. Buddies take turns choosing words, filling the squares, and guessing until no words remain. This activity helps students match the characteristics of letters to the configuration of words.

Letter Sounds and Clusters

Students should know that spoken words are made up of sounds or phonemes and should be able to segment words into those sounds. This is called phonemic awareness. For example, when a student hears the word *cat*, he should be able to identify three separate phonemes—kh/ah/t/. He should also know what *cat* means. (Remember, as explained in Chapter 2, it is made up of one morpheme or meaning unit.) Don't confuse phonemic awareness with phonics. Phonics involves knowing that sounds can be represented with printed letters, whereas phonemic awareness involves hearing separate sounds. To learn to read, one needs to possess phonemic awareness and some basic phonics knowledge. For students who have literacy experiences at home, this knowledge is often intuitive. For others, these concepts may need to be introduced and practiced in a variety of ways.

To use letter sounds and clusters (i.e., groups of letters that are pronounced together) to unlock difficult words, all students, especially struggling readers and English learners, need some ability to:

◎ Break words into phonemes.

◎ Remove a sound from a word.

◎ Isolate sounds at the beginning, middle, or end of a word.

◎ Create rhyming words.

◎ Tap out syllables.

The next two strategies call attention to sound and structure, thereby building phonemic awareness and basic phonics skills. When you implement these strategies, be sure to define each new word and use it in a sentence students can understand, to help them connect meaning to the word.

◎ **Stretch-a-Word** trains the ears to stretch out a word as if stretching a rubber band between two fingers, allowing students to hear its beginning, middle, and end sounds. In fact, the first time you do this activity, you might want to use a rubber band. For example, write *butterfly* on the chalkboard. As you say each part of the word clearly, stretch the rubber band from the *b* to the *y*. Next, have students stretch an imaginary rubber band between their fingers as they say *butterfly*, and other words themselves.

◎ **Sound Boxes** help students separate the sounds in a word, which helps them learn to blend sounds and substitute one sound for another to make a new word. To make a Sound Box, outline a word's phonemes to let students see and hear the breaks in words. (See sample next page.) Then encourage students to create their own Sound Boxes with words they choose.

◆ Use both Stretch-a-Word and Sound Boxes when you introduce new words in reading, spelling, or the content areas so students can focus on the meaning and structure of new words.

Sound Boxes help students identify individual sounds in words. ▶

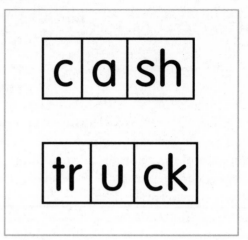

Letter "Chunks"

Letter "chunks" are common groups of letters that are easy to recognize, for example *-ack*, *-ide*, and *-ore*. Once students can isolate and blend sounds, you can help them learn to identify these chunks or phonograms. A phonogram is a group of letters that makes the same sound whenever they appear in a word. (See chart below.) When you add a letter at the beginning of a phonogram, you create a word. For example, when you add *d*, *g*, *n*, and *s* to *-ame*, you create the word family *dame*, *game*, *name* and *same*. Thirty-seven word families consisting of 500 one-syllable words can be created from the 37 phonograms in the chart below (Blevins, 1998).

Students can create nearly 500 words from these 37 phonograms. ▶

ack	ap	est	ing	ore
ail	ash	ice	ink	uck
ain	at	ick	ip	ug
ake	ate	ide	ir	ump
ale	aw	ight	ock	unk
ame	ay	ill	oke	
an	eat	in	op	
ank	ell	ine	or	

The next six strategies help you build students' awareness of phonograms in particular and word structure in general. Remember always to connect word meanings to word structure so that students gain a richer understanding of the words they are learning.

◎ **Flip Books** are a way to focus students' attention on common letter patterns and word families. To make a flip book, staple 6 to 10 sheets of same-size paper to one sheet that is about 3 inches longer. On the exposed part of the longer sheet, have students write a rime such as *-ame*, *-ore*, or *-unk*. On each of the shorter sheets, have them write an onset and draw a picture to represent each word they create. (See sample below.)

Once students can substitute individual letter sounds, you can help them identify groups of letters or clusters, such as *bl, sl, tr, pr, str*. Then they can add words such as *blame* and *shame* to the *-ame* word family. When students flip the pages of these little books, they learn a lot: They practice letter substitution to create words, become familiar with rhyming words, and connect pictures to words. Published flip books are also available, such as *Mitten/Kitten* by Jerome Martin (Trumpet).

Flip Books reinforce word families like this one for -ame.

◎ **Clap-It** is a strategy that focuses on splitting multisyllabic words into "chunks" by clapping or tapping out syllables. The ability to identify component parts of a word in this way builds awareness of sound structure. When students hear syllables in words, such *cal-en-dar* or *trust-wor-thy*, they begin to look for these chunks when they read them in print.

Another way students can learn words is by finding a small word in a big word, for instance *part* in *particular*. Often, though, the small word is not pronounced as it is in the longer word, for example *an* in *language* and *our* in *encourage*, which can lead to confusion. But even so, when words are chosen carefully, this strategy often gives clues to meaning, as with *drama* and *dramatically*.

Internet Connection

www.downline.co.uk/
fun/anagrams/

This site teaches about little words found in big words and shows how to create anagrams.

© **Spelling Cheerleading** elicits visual, auditory, and kinesthetic responses to words by drawing students' attention to letter shapes and word structure (Rogers, 1999). For this activity, students stand and "spell" words with their bodies—by touching their toes for letters with descenders such as *y* or *p*; stretching their hands above their heads for letters with ascenders such as *d* or *b*; and putting their hands on their waists for letters with neither, such as *a* or *e*. (See chart below for the body position of each letter.) As such, it sensitizes students to the way words look. When students "cheerlead" a list of words from two or three different word families, such as *-ame*, *-ape*, or *-and*, they begin to sort words according to similar letter patterns. You can have your class stand and "cheerlead" a list of words from the blackboard. And, you can have individual students "cheerlead" a word from the list for others to guess. This activity not only reinforces letter shapes and sequences, but also accommodates different learning styles.

(b, d, f, h, k, l, and t)

(a, c, e, i, m, n, o, r, s, u, v, w, x, and z)

(g, j, p, q, and y)

The three body positions for Spelling Cheerleading

◎ **Making Words** is a small-group or individual activity in which students manipulate letter cards to create two- to five-letter words, leading to a final word that contains all the letters (Cunningham & Cunningham, 1992). It is a hands-on way to help students discover sound-letter relationships and patterns in words.

PREPARING FOR THE LESSON:

◆ Choose a final word, such as *computer*, taking into consideration the number of vowels it contains, curriculum connections, and letter-sound patterns.

◆ List the two-, three-, four-, five-, and six-letter words you can make from this word.

◆ Pick 12 to15 words from the list and organize them in different ways:

a. words with similar patterns: *cope, rope, mope; more, tore, pore, core, cut, rut*

b. little words: *to, cup, put*

c. bigger words: *prom, compute*

d. words with the same letters in different places: *rope, pore*

e. proper names: *Tom*

f. words most students have in their listening vocabularies: *top, crop, toe, more*

◆ Write these words on index cards, ordering them from shortest to longest and grouping them by letter pattern.

◆ Put each letter of the word on an index card. Print consonants in black and vowels in red to distinguish the two and help students more easily see letter patterns. (If you do this activity with small groups, make enough letter-card sets for each member. Put each set on different-colored index cards to make it easier to sort cards at the end.)

◆ Store all cards in an envelope. Write on the envelope the words that can be made and the patterns you will sort for at the end.

"Computer"

2	3	4	5	6
to	cut	cope	cuter	compute
me	rut	rope		
up	put	mope		
	cup	more		
	Tom	tore		
	top	pore		
	cop	core		
	mop	prom		
	toe	crop		
		cute		
		come		
		pout		
		rout		

▲ *Many small words can be made from "computer."*

CARRYING OUT THE LESSON:

Gather the student or students around you and give each a set of letter cards. Hold up each card in a set, naming each letter and having students do the same. Make a two-letter word for them on a chalk ledge, pocket chart, or table top, and write the word on the chalkboard. Again, have students repeat what you do. Then have them make other two-letter words and say them aloud as you add them to the list on the board. Continue with three- and four-letter words, giving students clues when they have trouble. Before telling them the final word, ask them to guess what it might be and try to make it.

Once students have made all the words they can and you have added them to the list, put the index cards on which you have written words on the chalk ledge one at a time. Then review the words the students made, asking them to say each word with you. Now, have students sort these words according to spelling patterns and point out particular patterns. Then have students spell a few words they have not made cards for that contain one or more of these spelling patterns.

With younger children, Cunningham and Cunningham (1992) suggest using words such as *trunks, sports, spends, splash, scratch, tricks, turned, turtles, chapter, carrots, plate, sturdy, bathtubs, friends, panther, kittens, steam, present,* and *strange.* Your students can make many smaller words from each of these words.

On $8\frac{1}{2}$ x 11" paper, photocopy letters in a big word, such as "continents," for students to cut out.

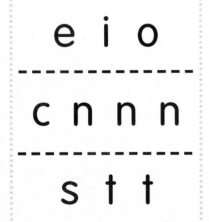

◎ **Making BIG Words** is a Making Words activity for older students that third-grade teacher Pat Kollar adapted. She chooses a big word (BW) to correlate with a topic she is covering in class, such as *continents.* Here are her suggestions for carrying out the activity:

◈ Give each student a copy of the BW letters printed on an $8\frac{1}{2}$ x 11" sheet. (See sample left.) Have them underline letters so they can tell a *u* from an *n,* a *p* from a *b,* and so forth.

◈ Have students cut out the letters, separate them into vowels and consonants, and line them up across the tops of their desks in alphabetical order.

◈ Give each student a piece of blank paper.

◈ Set a timer for 3 to 4 minutes (or longer as your students become more proficient). Have students make words by manipulating the letters, writing down each one on paper. If they figure out the BW, have them write it at the bottom of their paper. (See Megan's list on page 79.)

◈ After 3 to 4 minutes, go around the room and have each student name a word from his or her list, beginning with small words and moving to bigger ones.

◆ Record the words on chart paper, listing words according to the number of letters in them. Engage students in a discussion of word families, letter patterns, vowel combinations, consonant blends, and so forth. Challenge them to find words whose letters can be rearranged to spell new words, for example *tone* and *note*.

◆ Have students manipulate letters to see if they can discover the BW. Cunningham and Cunningham (1992) suggest using longer words such as *alphabetical, earthquakes, generation, instruments, motorcycles, temperature,* and *woodpecker* with older students.

Pat includes a BW in the class's weekly spelling list. She also puts the words students created (as well as some they didn't think of) into a "Making Big Words Center." Tasks at the center reinforce learning words by requiring students to use them in a variety of ways. For example, Pat encourages students to write "expensive" sentences containing the words ("I felt very proud when I won first prize in the baking <u>contest</u>."), rather than "cheap" ones ("I won the <u>contest</u>.") to extend their written vocabulary and creativity. (See sample next page.)

Making BIG Words is extremely popular with Pat's students. She says

in			
tin	tins		stone
one	none	once	Content
on			Contents
ton	tons		
tone	cone		
tent	tents		
sent			
scent			
not			
cot	cots		
sit	sits		
nest			
cent	cents		

Megan made this list of words from "continents."

(See sample next page.)

Making Big-Words Tasks

◎ Order words from smallest to biggest on pocket chart.

◎ Say and spell each word on the pocket chart. (Use your proofreader finger to touch each letter as you say it.)

◎ Order words by letter family and record them on paper.

◎ Spell more family words by adding other letters or endings.

◎ Choose eight words and write them in ABC order.

◎ Choose five other words and write five "expensive sentences."

Internet Connection

http://netnet.net/
~jgales/wrdsites.html

This site offers a variety of links to good "word" sites, many of which offer fun games. For example, "What's in a Name?" gives students two minutes to make as many words as they can using the letters in a name, and "Susie's Place" includes word games such as "Crambo," "Doggerel," and "Stinky Pinky."

"They look forward to the lessons, and I enjoy teaching them. Sometimes, for homework, I give the class the Big Words sheet for the BW of the day, and encourage parents to participate. (See sample below.) The students cut out the letters at home and manipulate them to make words that they write on the Big Words sheet. They love to challenge their parents to find the BW that they already know."

ABC order

1. cents
2. content
3. contents
4. once
5. scent
6. stone
7. tents
8. tins

- -

"Expensive Sentences"

1. cents - I gave her 25¢ (cents) for the ring and she gave me back 3¢ (cents). It cost 22¢.

2. content - My cat is content to sleep all day but she plays all night with me.

3. contents - My science book has a long Table of Contents.

4. once - _____

_____

5. scent - _____

Using these worksheets, Megan alphabetized her words, used them in "expensive sentences," and organized them by word family and number of letters.

BIG WORDS

Word Family -in
1. tin
2. sin
3. _____
4. _____

Word Family -ent
1. tent
2. sent
3. cent
4. scent

Word Family -one
1. tone
2. cone
3. stone
4. _____

Word Family _____
1. _____
2. _____
3. _____
4. _____

4 letter words	five letter words	six (or more) letter words
none	scent	contest
once	stone	contents
	scent	
	tents	
	cents	

The BIG word is continents .

◎ **Word Sorts** is a fun activity that helps students focus on word features, associations, and meanings to improve their vocabulary and spelling. Students can do sorts individually, in pairs, or in small groups, looking for common attributes in words and then categorizing and classifying them. Sorting promotes critical thinking and creativity. Follow these steps:

◈ **Identify words you want to reinforce and write each on an index card.** You can use any category or categories of words, but it is always a good idea to have some words in the group that don't fit, to challenge your students to think about novel ways of classifying the words. Words can come from students' reading, writing, and spelling, and should include mainly words they know, but a few they don't know, too.

Focus on word meaning and word structure with this activity. Some categories to consider:

- letter clusters and blends
- vowel/consonant patterns
- syllables
- parts of speech
- plurals
- common roots
- word families
- proper nouns
- words on a theme or topic

Regardless of sorting criteria, keep the number of words small enough so students are not overwhelmed, perhaps as few as six words for younger, struggling, or ESL learners. As they get better at sorting, they will be able to handle a larger number of words. Write each word on an index card.

◈ **Model a Word Sort for students.** Put each word out on a desktop or chalk ledge and use it in

Words sorted according to meaning and structure

couch	neighbor	closet
television	window	clothes
computer	garden	robe
chair	squirrel	slippers
		bed
	lamp	dream
	stamp	

a sentence. Then sort the words into groups, explaining to students what you're doing as you go: "All these words are pieces of furniture." "These words are things I can see from my kitchen." "These words have the same letters, -amp." "All these words are things you would find in my bedroom." (See sample on previous page.)

Explain to students that there are many ways to sort words, and to resort them into completely different categories, then show them how: "*Computer, chair,* and *neighbor* all end in *r.*" "*Closet, clothes, slippers, dream,* and *stamp* all begin with a two-letter cluster." You can also ask them to guess why you sorted words a particular way, offering clues if they have trouble. Be sure to accept all answers that make sense.

◆ **Have students do Word Sorts on their own.** Once students are familiar with Word Sorts, they can do their own, individually or in small groups. Encourage sorts that focus on concepts, such as "things we use in the house" or "things we do," and not just letters, sounds, or letter patterns, to promote an understanding of word meanings, word associations, critical thinking, and creativity. Be sure to observe them carefully to gather assessment information about their word knowledge.

Compound words are wonderful for Word Sorts. Putting little words together to make a bigger word, for example, *snow + man, butter + fly, bed + room,* and *cook + book,* helps students understand how word meaning is created. By making compound words, they also come to understand word "chunks" and syllables. It's fun to see how many compound words can be made from one small word, for example:

- *some* (someone, sometime, bothersome, somewhere, somebody, somehow)
- *any* (anytime, anyone, anyhow, anybody, anywhere, anyway)
- *time* (sometime, anytime, noontime, daytime, nighttime)

◆ **Create a classroom Word Sort Center.** Consider a center in the classroom where students work independently or with a buddy. Have them write down their sorts and check each other's work for accuracy. Keep color-coded cards in matching envelopes to facilitate clean-up.

Prefixes, Roots, and Suffixes

Besides knowing about letter chunks, knowing about prefixes, suffixes, and root (or base) words helps students learn words. Prefixes and suffixes often change a word's meaning and form. For example *invent*, a verb, becomes a noun when *-ion* is added to it (*invention*). *Believe*, a verb, becomes an adverb when *-able* is added to it (*believable*). Teaching students to recognize these chunks gives them an important tool for unlocking and learning new multisyllabic words. It also gives them a big advantage when they meet these words in reading and want to use them in writing.

Prefixes

Prefixes are letter groups that come before a root word to give it a new meaning. Here are ten of the most commonly taught prefixes, their definitions, and some examples. The first three prefixes appear most frequently in English.

It is important to teach students the meanings of these and other prefixes they meet during reading. For example, knowing that *anti-* means "against" helps students unlock *antibiotic* and *antifreeze*, knowing that *im-* means "not" helps unlock *immobile* and *immoderate*, and knowing that *mis-* means "wrong" or "bad" helps unlock *mistake* and *misbehave*. Knowing meanings for prefixes gives students a strategy for figuring out words independently.

Most Common Prefixes

PREFIX	DEFINITION	EXAMPLE
re-	again	*review, revoke*
un-	not	*unable, untrue*
in-	into or not	*insight, inert*
en-	in, put into	*enliven, ensnare*
ex-	out	*exit, extinguish*
de-	away, from	*deflect, denounce*
com-	together, with	*commune, communicate*
dis-	apart	*dishonest, disagree*
pre-	before	*prevent, predict*
sub-	under	*submerge, submarine*

Roots

Roots are base words to which prefixes and suffixes are attached. Roots consistently mean the same thing and are the base for related words. Students often meet roots of Greek and Latin origin in science. For example, it's no coincidence that *astro-*, the Greek word for *star*, is the root word of *astronomer*, *astronaut*, *astrology*, and *astrolabe*. Teach your students common roots like this and show them how adding prefixes and suffixes to them

Internet Connection

www.funbrain.
com/verb/index.html

This site gives practice with using verbs correctly.

creates new, but related words. Here some commonly taught root words, their definitions, and examples:

Most Common Roots

Root	Definition	Example
tract	drag, pull	*tractor, distract*
spect	look	*inspect, spectacle*
port	carry	*portable, important*
dict	say	*diction, dictionary, prediction*
rupt	break	*interrupt, rupture*
scrib	write	*inscribe, describe, scripture*
cred	believe	*credit, discredit*
vid	see	*video, evidence*
aud	hear	*audience, auditorium, audible*

Suffixes

Suffixes are letter groups added after a root word to give it a new meaning. Often suffixes change the word's tense and form. Young readers first learn common endings such as *-s, -er, -est, -ed, -ing, -less,* and *-ly*. Here are a few everyday suffixes, their definitions, and some examples to teach your students. The first four suffixes appear most frequently in English:

Most Common Suffixes

Suffix	Definition	Example
-ly	having the quality of	*lightly, sweetly, weekly*
-er	more	*higher, stronger, smoother*
-able/-ible	able to	*believable, deliverable, incredible*
-tion/-sion	a thing, a noun	*invention, suspension, tension, function*
-cle	small	*particle*
-less	without	*treeless, motionless*
-est	most	*biggest, hardest, brightest*
-less	without	*fearless, headless, careless*
-ment	quality or act	*contentment, excitement, basement*
-ness	quality or act	*kindness, wildness, softness*
-arium	a place for	*aquarium, terrarium*
-ling	small	*duckling, gosling, hatchling*

@ **Vocabulary Squares** is a visual-verbal word association strategy that focuses students' attention on prefixes and roots, helping them to create personal associations in picture form for unfamiliar words as they learn them. Hopkins and Bean (1999) found this strategy helped develop the "independent problem-solving skills" of junior-high and high-school students on the Northern Cheyenne Reservation in southeastern Montana.

To introduce the strategy, draw a square and divide it into four smaller squares. In the top-left square, write the prefix to be taught, for example *sub-*, and the dictionary definition in the square below, for example *under*. (See sample below.) Then, in the top-right square, write a word that has the prefix, for example *submarine*, and its definition, *a boat that goes under water*. In the bottom-right square, draw a picture of the word.

Model a few Vocabulary Squares for students, and then guide them as they practice the strategy on their own. Students can copy your models into their vocabulary notebooks as a reference. You can also give Vocabulary Squares as homework or a classroom assignment that students complete one or two days a week. Have students collect words that share the same prefix or root, and post lists in the classroom. (See Appendix, page 126.) That way everyone sees the range of words containing the same letter chunks. Remember to tell students that the goal of the strategy is not just to help them learn the meanings of roots and prefixes, but for them to use this knowledge to figure out and learn new words.

Vocabulary Squares help a seventh grader learn various aspects of new words.

Prefix	Defined
sub-	submarine: a boat that goes under water
under	
Definition	**Drawing**

Root	Defined
spect-	spectator: someone who watches but doesn't take part
watch or behold	
Definition	**Drawing**

@ **A Root a Week** is a week-long activity that builds students' knowledge of Greek and Latin roots and affixes, and enables them to discern and analyze meanings of words. Janine Federowicz says, "Learning these important word parts should not be left to middle or high school. I teach them to my third graders." Begin by choosing a bulletin board large enough for a picture of a tree with spreading branches and a root system. (See sample on next page.) Then follow these steps:

◆ **MONDAY** Decide the root, prefix, or suffix your students will learn for the week, for example, *geo-* (meaning *earth*), and write it at the base of one of the tree's branches. Ask students for words they know that contain *geo-* and write them on or near that branch. From the words students supply, see if they can figure out the meaning of *geo-*. If they can't, supply it for them. Have students write the root and sample words in their notebooks. For homework on Monday night, have them check with family members, listen to TV, or use the dictionary to find more words that contain the root and write them in their notebooks.

◆ **TUESDAY** Have students write all the *geo-* words they came up with on the tree near the *geo-* branch. Depending on how many words they generate, divide the class into small groups and, for homework, have each group define a few of the words by looking them up, asking someone, or drawing conclusions based on parallels they see in the sample words.

◆ **WEDNESDAY** Have students share their definitions with the class, for example, a *geoduck* is *a very large, burrowing edible clam* (*Webster's New World College Dictionary, second edition*, 1997). Encourage students to add their classmates' words to their notebooks. For homework, have student pick five words and use them in sentences or write a story or poem using them.

◆ **THURSDAY** Have students share their sentences, stories, and poems in small groups or with the whole class. If you have time, ask students to act out their words.

◆ **FRIDAY** Do a quick assessment of students' knowledge of the words by either providing definitions and asking students to supply the correct word or vice versa.

◆ **MONDAY** Select a new root, prefix, or suffix that appears commonly such as *demo* (people), *mal* (bad), or *mag* (good) and begin the process again.

If you don't have the bulletin board space for the large tree, give your students blank copies of the "Word Tree" in the Appendix, page 127, and have them record words they find containing common roots or affixes. These sheets can be kept in three-ring binders for review and reference during writing. Students often dislike looking words up in the dictionary, but Root a Week gives them independent strategies for figuring out new and difficult words on their own. Janine says, "I was a high school freshman before I learned the Greek and Latin roots that helped me understand why the evil woman in Disney's *Sleeping Beauty* was named *Malificent*. Now, my third graders understand that *mal-* means 'bad' and they can understand other words like *malevolent* and *malicious*."

A "Root" a Week Tree

geoponic *geodesic*
geological *geology*
geomorphic *geography* *geometric mean*
geode *geomagnetic* *geoduck*
geomorphology *geophysics*
geometry
geo- (earth)

You can use words from your language arts, science, or social studies curriculum. Have students use colored markers to distinguish one word family from another on the tree or draw large leaves on the branches to hold the words students contribute. They can also circle the targeted roots or affixes to further reinforce them. If you teach Root a Week, you'll have a full tree in a month or two (depending on how large your bulletin board is).

For more classroom-tested ideas to help your students develop decoding, spelling, fluency, and word meanings, consult *Classrooms That Work: They Can All Read and Write*, second edition, by Patricia Cunningham and Richard Allington (Longman, 1999).

▲

Creating a Root a Week gives students independent strategies for unlocking multi-syllabic words.

Hit or Miss promotes knowledge of correct spelling, letter "chunks," and key curriculum vocabulary. Mary Kunzman and Mary Higham, who adapted this strategy from *The Mailbox* (1998), use Hit or Miss with third graders, but it can be used at other grade levels too.

Select 10 to 12 science or social studies words or spelling words. Distribute copies of the Hit or Miss grid. (See sample below and Appendix, page 128.) Words on the grid come from a study of penguins and the book *Playing with Penguins and Other Adventures in Antarctica* by Ann McGovern (Scholastic). Have each student copy the words from a list you provide, writing them randomly in the boxes. With 24 boxes, there will be variation in where the words appear. Divide the class into pairs. Player #1 calls out a set of coordinates, such as C-4 or B-2. If Player #2 has a word in that box, she says "Hit," uses the word in a sentence, and listens to Player #1 spell the word. If it is correctly spelled, the box gets crossed off. If it's not spelled correctly, it is then Player #2's turn. If the box is blank, Player #2 says "Miss," and it's his turn to call out a set of coordinates. The game continues until one person has crossed off all his or her spelling words. Some variations include:

····· Hit or Miss ·····

	A	B	C	D	E	F
⑤		tuxedos			glaciers	
④	pancake ice			emperor		
③	rookery		penguins		seals	
②		icebergs			Antarctica	
①				whales		sea lion

▲

Use Hit or Miss grids in the classroom or for homework, to promote correct spelling and key curriculum vocabulary.

◆ Use names, holidays, or seasonal or functional vocabulary from your community, such as restaurant names, public sites, or points of interest. Use words from a book you are reading to your class to help students transfer reading and listening vocabulary to writing vocabulary.

◆ Occasionally, gather students into groups of three and four, but no larger. (Playing with the whole class takes longer.)

◆ Send two copies of the Hit or Miss grid home as homework so parents can play with their child.

◆ Make copies of the grid accessible so pairs of students can choose words and play during center time or when their work is complete.

◆ Invite students to make up their own rules for variations of the game.

◆ Let students use colored markers as a motivator for neat writing and accurate spelling.

Hit or Miss builds awareness of the structure and spelling of new and difficult words and lets students connect meanings to them. Of course, the object is to spell all the words correctly. Mary encourages students to help each other remember spellings and meanings.

◎ **Rivet** is a pre-reading strategy that focuses students' attention on the way letters go together to make a word (Cunningham, Hall, & Cunningham, 2000). It requires students to use prior knowledge and make predictions, thus increasing their involvement in reading and boosting their comprehension. Teachers who use this strategy find their students' attention is "riveted" on the activity. Here are the steps:

◆ Pre-read the story or selection you plan to share with the class and choose six to eight words that seem difficult, but are important to understanding the text. You can include characters' names or phrases.

◆ As the class watches, draw lines on the blackboard to represent each letter in each word. Prepare a similar handout for students or have them make their own.

◆ Tell students you'd like them to try to guess each new word as you supply the letters.

◆ Fill in each word by supplying one letter at a time. Pause after writing each letter to see if anyone can guess the word. When someone guesses it, have the class finish spelling it.

◆ Once you've written out all the words, define them and invite students to predict some of the events in the story using these words.

You can model Rivet by giving students as much or as little information as you think they need about the text they will read in order to guess the new words. For example, to introduce a book like *Amelia and Eleanor* by Pam Ryan (Scholastic), you can tell students it is a story about two famous women, Amelia Earhart, a pilot, and Eleanor Roosevelt, a president's wife, who had dinner in the White House and then took a plane ride together. Explain that you read the story and found some words that are important for them

to know. On the blackboard, write numbered lines for the letters of each word (e.g., *aviator*, *First Lady*, "*birds of a feather*"). Have students do the

Internet Connection

www.funbrain.com
www.eduplace.com

These fun sites offer students word searches and puzzles, with vocabulary organized by topic or theme.

www.puzzlemaker.com

Puzzlemaker.com lets students create their own crossword puzzles and word searches.

same on paper. Then, supply the first few letters of the first word, one at a time, until there are enough letters so that students can guess the word. If they are right, have them finish spelling it.

1. a v i a t _ _ _
2. _ _ _ _ _ _ _ _ _
3. _ _ _ _ _ _ _ _
  _ _ _ _ _ _ _

Next, supply the first few letters of the two-word phrase until students can guess it. Then have them finish spelling it.

1. a v i a t o r
2. f i r s _ _ _ _ _
3. _ _ _ _ _ _ _ _
  _ _ _ _ _ _ _

As more letters are guessed, and you fill in the blanks, students should begin to see what the target word is. If they don't, give clues such as "This word describes someone who is a pilot," "These words describe someone who lives in the White House," and "This phrase describes things that are the same." If students give a wrong guess, keep supplying letters or clues until they identify all the words. Then invite students to make predictions about events in the story using the new words. Follow up by reading the story or selection to see if their predictions are accurate.

Rivet is also effective as a pre-reading activity for science or social studies, to help students with technical vocabulary. Keep in mind, though, that when multisyllabic words are the focus, students who know some affixes and roots will have an easier time. As students try to supply the letters for a new science word like *photosynthesis* or a new social studies word like *globalization*, Rivet not only helps them learn a word's meaning, but its pronunciation and spelling as well. Once students identify a new word, you can reinforce roots like *synth-* and *globe-* and affixes like *photo-*, *-sis*, and *-tion*. Encourage students, for example, to supply other words in the *synth-* and *globe-* families.

Property Posters is an idea Tracy Ryan-D'Arpino uses with her middle-school students to reinforce the definitions of the five multiplication properties (associative, commutative, distributive, identity, and zero). Understanding these concepts is basic to improving students' math sense and computation skills. After she has taught each of the properties over several days, Tracy introduces this activity by asking some "strange" math questions and getting students' "just for fun" answers. She says she gets students' attention and creative responses to these questions but the real answers improve students' understanding of patterns and numbers. Here are some examples:

> **Q:** "Why would an eight associate with a five instead of a seven?"
>
> **A:** "It's easy to count by five's" or "He likes the number 13."
>
> **Q:** "When told she could increase herself, why do you think 56 chose to multiply herself by 1?"
>
> **A:** "She really hates change" or "She isn't very smart."

Then, Tracy writes the terms for the five multiplication properties on the chalkboard and defines them orally, giving students examples that illustrate each one, for example "In multiplication, the eight can associate with the five or the seven and you get the same result: $(8 \times 5) \times 7 = 8 \times (5 \times 7)$."

Next, she has students use classroom dictionaries, as well as their own background knowledge, to find root words and their definitions. Once students verify or paraphrase the original definitions, she records and reviews them with the class:

- **ASSOCIATIVE** (associate—to group with) The way factors are grouped doesn't change the product, for example $6 \times (9 \times 2) = (6 \times 9) \times 2$.

- **COMMUTATIVE** (commute—to be interchangeable) The order of the factors doesn't change the product, for example $2 \times 3 = 3 \times 2$.

- **DISTRIBUTIVE** (distribute—to spread out) Multiplying a sum by a number is the same as multiplying each addend by that number, for example $19 \times 4 = (10 \times 4) + (9 \times 4)$.

- **IDENTITY** (one) When a number is multiplied by one, the product stays the same, for example $15 \times 1 = 15$.

- **ZERO** (nothing) When a number is multiplied by zero, the product is always zero, for example $15 \times 0 = 0$.

Tracy gives examples that are rich in words and numbers: "To *associate* means 'to group with.' The associative property of multiplication states that the way factors are grouped doesn't change the product. An example is 6 x (9 x 2) = (6 x 9) x 2." She also encourages discussion of each property with thought-provoking questions such as, "Can you describe how each expression gives the same product?" "Why is it easier for some of us to mentally multiply the second expression than the first one?"

Finally, Tracy asks students to create posters for each property, containing its definition, an example, and an illustration. She says, "The kids can be so creative, and sharing posters gives the class a sounder understanding of the five multiplication properties." (See sample left.) After this activity, Tracy displays Property Posters on bulletin boards so students can refer to them as they work.

DISTRIBUTIVE

One operation can be distributed over another and the results are always the same.

$$(4 \times 9) + (4 \times 10)$$

◆ ◆ ◆ ◆

S U M M A R Y

Being immersed in a word-rich environment and using language to learn are probably the best ways to increase vocabulary. But paying attention to the structure of words—knowing how letters go together to make words—is also important. Knowing the sounds of letters and letter clusters; being able to identify prefix, root, and suffix "chunks"; and learning how to manipulate words to make new words is important for stretching vocabulary. By using the strategies in this chapter, you can give students opportunities to focus on structure and use their knowledge to build huge vocabularies. In the next chapter, I will show you ways to encourage students to apply word-learning strategies independently.

Investigating Words

OF COURSE, THE ULTIMATE GOAL OF TEACHING
vocabulary is to help students become independent word learners.
We want our students to acquire "a personal repertoire of
independent strategies for negotiating meaning" (Harmon, Hedrick, & Fox,
2000). The activities in this book are stepping stones to that goal. So use
them only until students have mastered the strategies they're designed to
teach. Spending time practicing what students already know is time poorly
spent. Instead, use that time for reading, writing, and speaking—having
students apply their knowledge of words to communicate effectively.

Now that you have a good understanding of sound word-learning
practices, let's look at some ideas for encouraging students to apply word-
learning strategies independently in different contexts. Investigating words
with your students is a fun and effective way to help them learn new words
on their own. You can do this in several ways:

◎ Engage in wordplay. Also, read books to and with your students that play
with words.

◎ Use print resources such as the dictionary, thesaurus, and glossary, and
online resources to support students on their journey to becoming
independent "word solvers."

◎ Stretch your students' schemas for words through writing and
investigating literature.

**Internet
Connection**

www.surfnetkids.com/
wordgames.htm

This site contains a
host of "vocabulary
stretching" games for
upper-elementary and
middle-school students
and offers links to other
"word sites" on the Net
as well.

Wordplay

Wordplay means focusing on language in a lighthearted, lively way. Incorporating activities and materials into your teaching that use language playfully can have a dramatic effect on your students' word learning.

◎ **Wordplay Books** feature language and language patterns that are unique and humorous. Reading them to and with your students and making them available in your classroom are good ways to show how words work. For instance, in the story *Miss Alaineus: A Vocabulary Disaster* a fifth-grade girl named Sage (i.e., "one who shows wisdom, experience, and judgment") writes an imaginative definition for *miscellaneous*, without checking it in the dictionary. Then, during a vocabulary bee at school, she is "devastated, ruined, and finished" when she gives her definition. The author, Debra Fraiser, uses words in clever ways. For example, sentences run along the bottom or side of each page, containing vocabulary words from A to Z. ("*Obliterate* me, send me to *oblivion*—no one could *outdo* my stupidity.") This story benefits students of all ages because it explores word meanings in a lighthearted way.

The box on page 95 includes riddle books, joke books, poetry, alphabet books, autograph rhymes, and just-for-fun stories. Share them during read-aloud or when you have just a few minutes. Or pair students to read to each other. These books make excellent models to help students create their own wordplays.

Here are three ideas that encourage word-play:

◎ **Grandiloquence** means "*grand or pompous speech or expression.*" It is related to *eloquent* and *loquacious* and derived from the Latin root "*grandis*" (grand) and "*loquor*" (speech). Sandy Gofran wants her sixth graders to become *grandiloquent* as they learn to use their schemas and intuition to identify words.

Sandy hooks her students on words by sharing regular features in popular periodicals with her students. For example, using the *Reader's Digest* section "It Pays to Increase Your Word Power," she has her students learn new words and test their knowledge of their meanings. She photocopies the local newspaper's weekly "Jumble" cartoon, which requires solving a puzzle by playing with the meanings of words and phrases. Working crossword puzzles also stretches her students' vocabularies. Sandy says, "Activities like these help students acquire an intuitive sense of word meanings. Once they have an intuitive sense of meaning, they can use it to get at the meaning of new words."

By an "intuitive" sense, Sandy means figuring out part of a word's meaning from its structure or the context in which it is used, and determining its complete meaning based on that information. For example, if a student is doing a crossword puzzle and needs to think of a seven-letter word that means *antediluvian*, he may be able to arrive at its

Wonderful Wordplay Books

- Go Hang a Salami! I'm a Lasagna Hog! And Other Palindromes by J. Agee (Farrar, Straus & Giroux)
- A Snake Is Totally Tail by J. Barrett (Atheneum)
- A Gaggle of Geese: The Collective Names of the Animal Kingdom by P. Browne (Atheneum)
- Yours Til the Banana Splits: 201 Autograph Rhymes by J. Cole and S. Clamenson (Morrow)
- Jamberry by B. Degen (Harper & Row)
- Miss Alaineus: A Vocabulary Disaster by D. Frasier (Harcourt Brace)
- A Chartreuse Leotard in a Magenta Limousine: And Other Words Named After People and Places by L. Graham-Barber (Hyperion)
- The King Who Rained by F. Gwynne (Dutton)
- A Chocolate Moose For Dinner by F. Gwynne (Dutton)
- The Sixteen Hand Horse by F. Gwynne (Prentice-Hall)
- Up, Up and Away: A Book About Adverbs by R. Heller (Scholastic)
- Kites Sail High: A Book About Verbs by R. Heller (Scholastic)
- A Cache of Jewels and Other Collective Nouns by R. Heller (Grossett & Dunlap)
- Cat, What is That? by T. Johnston (HarperCollins)
- Eat Your Words: A Fascinating Look at the Language of Food by C.F. Jones (Delacorte)
- Busy Buzzing Bumblebees and Other Tongue Twisters by A. Schwartz (HarperCollins)
- Baloney, Henry P. by J. Scieszka (Viking Penguin)
- Tyrannosaurus Wrecks: A Book of Dinosaur Riddles by N. Sterne (Crowell)
- The Grapes of Math by G. Tang (Scholastic)
- Eight Ate: A Feast of Homonym Riddles by M. Terban (Clarion)
- In a Pickle and Other Funny Idioms by M. Terban (Clarion)
- Too Hot to Hoot: Funny Palindrome Riddles by M. Terban (Clarion)
- Guppies in Tuxedos. Funny Eponyms by M. Terban (Clarion)
- Funny You Should Ask: How to Make up Jokes and Riddles With Wordplay by M. Terban (Clarion)
- Time to Rhyme: A Rhyming Dictionary (Wordsong)
- The Z was Zapped by C. Van Allsburg (Houghton Mifflin)
- Runaway Opposites by R. Wilbur (Harcourt Brace)
- Lewis Carroll's Jabberwocky by J.B. Zalben (Boyds Mills Press)

meaning if he knows that "*ante*" means "*before.*" If the student checks the dictionary for the definition of "*diluvian,*" he may find that it refers to the era before the biblical flood. He may remember that a "*deluge*" of water could be a flood or perhaps an "*onslaught*" of mail or complaints. From all of that information, he may infer that "*antediluvian*" means "*old*" and come up with the puzzle word, *archaic.* This ability to investigate origin and meaning of difficult words is a much more effective way to learn a new word than memorizing a definition.

Internet Connection

www.acronym finder.com/about. asp#what

This handy site lets you discover the full names for acronyms such as NASA and NATO.

Fingerspelling, based on the American sign language alphabet, helps students learn words.

◎ **Fingerspelling** is a way to play with words using sign language, a non-verbal form of communication. Not only does it reinforce vocabulary and spelling by requiring students to represent words physically, but it also teaches students sensitivity for people who have hearing impairments. Marcus Zumwalt uses it with his third graders and finds it works especially well with students who learn kinesthetically and need active engagement.

Initially, Marcus had little knowledge of sign language. He learned along with his students. Using a letter poster, the class practiced vowels and a few consonants so they could make words right away. (See chart below.) Each day, Marcus reviewed the signs that he had taught previously and introduced two or three new ones. He taught students how to sign their names; everyday words such as *hello*, *please*, *thank you*, and *lunch*; and phrases such as *read a book*, *I love you*, and *come help me*. His students were excited about learning to communicate with their hands. They eagerly practiced in class and, with the help of a photocopied alphabet sheet, at home with their families.

After a few weeks, when students had mastered the alphabet, Marcus began to use the signs during language arts. When he introduced a new word, he wrote the word, spelled it orally, signed it, and had the class repeat what he did. The students discussed definitions of words and invented their own simple hand motions for them, such as thumping on their chests for the word *courage*.

Saying, spelling, signing, and acting out vocabulary words became regular practice. On some days the class had spelling bees where students signed and acted out definitions, in addition to spelling words orally. On other days they played games where one student signed a word and other students "read" the word. When students talked about a word, Marcus encouraged them to combine signing and hand motions with verbal spellings and pronunciations. Marcus found that by using these multiple strategies, his students scored higher on their spelling tests and showed greater enthusiasm for learning and using new words.

The beauty of signing is that, once students learn the

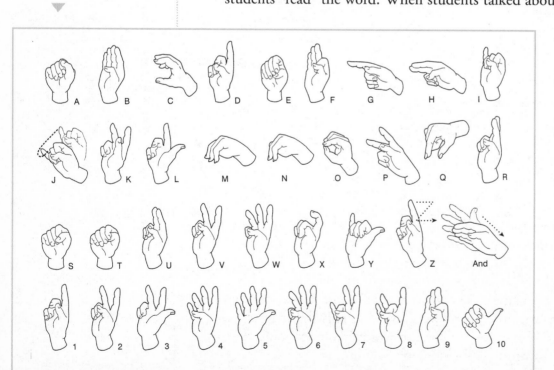

signs, incorporating them into daily spelling and vocabulary work takes little time. Students enjoy it because it is different and it allows them to actively construct words. Marcus says, "When my students translate a series of hand motions into a series of letters and then into a word, they go through several more mental steps than the average student ever does with a list of spelling words to memorize. And, the greatest thing is that the kids love doing it."

Marcus finds that his students sign words for spelling and vocabulary even when he doesn't require it of them. Now his only problem is the silent chatter of sign language across the classroom, which can be difficult to put to rest.

Using the Dictionary, Thesaurus, and Glossary

As students become more skilled writers and researchers, and read more challenging material for science and social studies, they often turn to resources for help with difficult words. Knowing how to use these resources well and feeling comfortable with them is important.

Of course, the dictionary and the thesaurus are good tools for stretching students' vocabularies. In earlier chapters, I covered several strategies that involve using the either or both. (See Chapter 2 for Word Webs, Concept Definition Maps, and Zooming In and Zooming Out; Chapter 3 for Guessed Meanings and Picture Dictionary; and Chapter 4 for A Root a Week and Vocabulary Squares.) In this chapter, you will find strategies that encourage students to use these resources independently in learning new words.

Unfortunately, the dictionary and thesaurus are not usually favorite references because of the time it takes to find a word. Electronic dictionaries and thesauruses have solved this problem to some extent, but students still resist using them. One

The Perfect Dictionary for Your Grade

These dictionaries are appropriate for students in grades 3–8:

◎ *The New Oxford Picture Dictionary: English/Spanish* by E. Parnwell (Oxford University Press) Ages 8–16

◎ *DK Merriam-Webster Children's Dictionary* (DK Publishing) Ages 9–12

◎ *Scholastic Visual Dictionary* (Scholastic) Ages 4–8

◎ *DK Children's Illustrated Dictionary* by J. McIlwain (DK Publishing) Ages 4–8

◎ *Scholastic Science Dictionary* by M. Berger (Scholastic) Ages 9–12

◎ *Scholastic Rhyming Dictionary* by S. Young (Scholastic) Ages 9–12

way to solve this is by teaching a lesson or two on how to use guide words, which can make accessing words in print references faster and easier.

First, make photocopies of a page from the dictionary and give each student a copy. Next, point out the guide words at the top of the page and tell students they are the "entrance" and "exit" to the page. Explain that by looking at only these two words—not searching the entire page—students can determine if the word they seek is on the page. Demonstrate this idea by naming several words and deciding together if they appear on the page.

Have students cover the page, leaving only the guide words showing. Pick a word at random and ask students to use the guide words to help them decide if the word occurs on, before, or after this page. Students quickly get the idea that using guide words can shorten the time it takes to look up words.

A thesaurus is a terrific resource for students as they search for vivid, precise language and, therefore, it is a must for every classroom. Most list synonyms and antonyms, but do not give definitions.

Introduce your students to the thesaurus with this riddle from *A First Thesaurus* by H. Wittels and J. Greisman: "What sounds like *Brontosaurus*, but is found on a bookshelf near the dictionaries, not at the natural history museum?" The answer is a *thesaurus*, of course. When students examine this 2,000-word thesaurus, they will see that the main word is in bold print, synonyms are in regular black, and antonyms are in red. Black-and-white illustrations are also included.

Talking about synonyms for a word sensitizes students to shades of its meaning. For example, *reliable, steady, unswerving, constant, unfailing,* and *regular* are synonyms for *consistent.* While *unswerving* can probably describe a boat's path, *unfailing* probably does not—certainly not as well as *steady* does. And students soon discover that although *joyful, glad, ecstatic, thrilled, contented,* and *pleased* are synonyms for *happy*, each one has a slightly different meaning that conveys a slightly different message. (See sample left.) As you help your students become aware of nuances in word meanings, you broaden their vocabularies and their power to use language effectively.

◀ *Third graders used a thesaurus and their own schemas to create a web of synonyms for "happy."*

The Perfect Thesaurus for Your Grade

These thesauruses are appropriate for students in grades 3 to 8:

- *A First Thesaurus* by H. Wittels and J. Greisman (Golden Books) Ages 5–9
- *The American Heritage Children's Thesaurus* by P. Hellweg (Houghton Mifflin) Ages 9–12
- *Roget's Children's Thesaurus* (Scott Foresman) Ages 9–12
- *Scholastic Child's Thesaurus* by J.K. Bollard (Scholastic) Ages 7–12

Internet Connection

www.merriam-webster.com

www.thesaurus.com

Check out these useful, easy-to-search online references.

Here are some ideas for creating and using references:

- **Pictionary-Dictionary**, a kind of personal dictionary, is a powerful tool for word learning. Typically, students keep a notebook of new words in which they spell the word, write its meaning, and draw a representative picture. Building a personal lexicon like this helps students take responsibility for their own word learning. For many students, their Pictionary-Dictionary is a resource for their writing and something to reread and add new illustrations to. For those who struggle with reading or who are learning English, it can build confidence by making vocabulary growth visible and concrete.

  Spiral bound notebooks make excellent Pictionary-Dictionaries. Or your students can make their own by stapling together colored tag board or wallpaper covers with blank or lined paper. Be sure to have them include at least one page for each letter of the alphabet. Have students look at a published dictionary before they put theirs together to help them decide on the format and length. Examining a dictionary closely shows students that more words in English begin with consonants than vowels, and some letters in the dictionary have much longer sections than others. Older students can use this information when they make their own dictionaries. Students can add page numbers, tabs for each letter, and a table of contents to make accessing words easy.

  Encourage students to add words from outside school, too—words they find when they are at home, on a trip, visiting relatives or friend, or out in the community. Depending on how quickly students fill their Pictionary-Dictionaries, you may want them to make one at the beginning of the year and another halfway through the year.

Students use Word Books to collect words that are important to them.

◎ **Word Books**, a type of "wearable" dictionary younger students enjoy keeping, builds students' personal lexicons using important words they encounter in their lives in and out of school. Barbara Regenspan, a professor of elementary education, says, "Children are walking collectors of language. They collect words from their experiences, and adults, siblings, and friends can help them add these words to their Word Books."

To create each book, Barbara says the teacher, older students, or parent volunteers can punch holes in 26 3 x 5" cards and bind them with shower curtain rings. (Variations include using 3 x 5" inch spiral notebooks or stapled sheets with tagboard covers.) She ties a 24" piece of yarn, ribbon, or string to each Word Book, so it can be worn around the neck. (See sample left.)

Barbara distributes the books to students and has them alphabetize the pages by writing upper- and lower-case letters on the top left-hand corner of each spread. The children fill in the words themselves, with an eye to spelling them correctly. They wear the books at home and at school so word learning is an independent out-of-school activity as well.

◎ **College Words** is a strategy Ann Goroleski uses to teach a new word a day, as she models using the dictionary. Her goal is to build her students' knowledge of interesting and colorful language so they can use it in their writing. She says, "The language my students use in their writing is surprisingly similar: 'Mom is pretty,' 'The dog is furry,' and 'People feel good (or bad, happy or sad).' College Words helps them use more precise language."

Ann chooses a new word a day from the dictionary, starting with A and moving forward alphabetically. She selects words she thinks will challenge her students, yet still be useful in their speaking and writing. Each day, she adds the chosen word to a chart of words she's covered on previous days. To introduce the word, she may say it and give its definition, or she may use the word in a sentence and have students infer its definition. Each day, after learning the new word, students review the whole list. When they have covered the entire alphabet, and listed 26 words, Ann engages them in follow-up activities in which she:

◆ Has students put words in their individual College Word dictionaries.

◆ Writes words on slips of paper and puts them into a bag. She then has each student pick a word and use it in a sentence.

◆ Chooses a word, gives only the definition, and has the class guess the word.

◆ Asks students to sort and classify the words according to different criteria, for example, parts of speech, number of syllables, theme.

◆ Invites students to write individual or group stories using as many of the new words as possible.

◆ Encourages students to look for the words in stories, the newspaper, on television, in school announcements, and so forth.

Over the years, Ann has called this activity Author Words, $100 Words, and College Words. But she says, "It doesn't matter what I call it. What matters is that, afterwards, I get stories in which 'Mom is *exquisite*,' 'The *canines* are furry,' and 'People feel *weary*, *cantankerous*, and *ambitious*.'"

⊚ **Snapshot Alphabet** is a project in which students create dictionaries made up of photographs they take. As they work independently to gather images from their surroundings, they not only learn about words, but also about other cultures. It's particularly helpful for young students, ESL learners, and struggling readers who are learning their ABCs. It builds community among diverse students as it builds vocabulary.

Jane Andrus got the idea for Snapshot Alphabet after one student's grandfather donated enough 26-exposure disposable cameras for the whole class. She introduced Snapshot Alphabet to her students by telling them they were going to make dictionaries by taking photographs of special objects, people, or events in their homes or their relatives' homes.

Before distributing the cameras, Jane held lessons to demonstrate the importance of lighting, posing subjects, knowing when to snap a photo, and holding the camera steady. She created a 26-line form to help students keep track of their photos, and capture an

As they take photos for Snapshot Alphabet, students record each frame by number.
▼

Aa Bb Cc Dd Ee Ff Gg Hh Ii Jj Kk Ll Mm Nn Oo Pp Qq Rr Ss Tt Uu Vv Ww Xx Yy Zz

1. Annie - Annie is my sister.

2. Bruno - Bruno is my dog.

3. football - My friends and me are playing football.

4. yard - This is the yard where we play.

5. wok - My mom cooks with a wok.

6. dumplings - These dumplings aren't my favorite food

7. noodles - I like to eat these noodles.

8. Stellar - This is me and that's my name.

9. calculator - I like to use my calculator.

10. Mom - My mom goes to work everyday.

11. Tom - Tom is my big brother (he is 9).

12. house - This is our house at 18 Cherry St.

Internet Connection

www.polaroid.com/
work/teachers/
workshops/index.jsp

This is the site for the Polaroid Education Program. It offers training programs and products to K–12 teachers that support visual learning and the use of instant, digital, and conventional photography in the classroom.

image for each letter. (See sample previous page.) After the lesson, Jane's students took home a plastic bag that held a camera, a letter to parents about the project, a record form, and instructions for taking snapshots.

When students brought the cameras back to school, Jane had the pictures developed. Students mounted their photos on 26 loose pages, heading each page with a letter of the alphabet. Under each photo, they wrote the word it represented and a sentence containing the word. Then they alphabetized their pages, added covers and a title page, and stapled their dictionaries together. Finally, the students read their dictionaries to the class, and put them in the classroom library for everyone to enjoy.

Here are some ways to adapt Jane's idea to your classroom:

- Focus on a theme, such as food. It's a great way to share and celebrate unique differences in families.

- Focus on words that are important in particular settings, such as a restaurant, library, bank, beauty parlor, or grocery store.

- Have ESL students write words in English and in their native tongue to help English-first speakers learn the ESL students' language and vice versa.

- Help students with special needs write words with yarn or beads, and then trace letter formations with their fingers to learn the words.

- Have older students read their Snapshot Alphabet albums to younger ones.

- Encourage students to use more than one word and one object for a letter, for example, "*Here is my uncle under an umbrella.*"

Jane says, "This project exposed students to different cultures and interesting vocabulary such as *mancala* and *wok*. For my students and me, it promoted word learning, reading and writing, and offered opportunities for us to discover how different and alike we all are."

Web-a-Word is a strategy Laurie McKeveney, a reading specialist, uses to encourage students to use the dictionary. Using a graphic organizer, Laurie teaches her students how to use prefixes, suffixes, and roots to figure out words they don't know. She starts with common prefixes, suffixes, and roots, such as those listed in Chapter 4, but moves on to more difficult ones once her students have mastered the common ones. Her goal is to have students use word parts to decode and define all kinds of words instantly, and use those words when they speak and write. She also wants them to be able to share their thinking with each other. This is how she does it:

(continued on page 104)

Less-Common Prefixes, Roots, and Suffixes

PREFIX	MEANING	EXAMPLE
anti-	opposite or before	*anticipate*
auto-	self	*automatic*
fore-	in front of	*forehand*
hyper-	over	*hyperactive*
inter-	between	*interview*
multi-	many	*multiple*
over-	above	*overwhelm*
pre-	before	*premeditate*
semi-	in part or partially	*semiconductor*
super-	over or above	*superficial*
tele-	transmit	*telephone*
trans-	across	*transatlantic*
under-	below	*undercover*

ROOT	MEANING	EXAMPLE
bios	life	*biosphere*
cardio	heart	*cardiac*
derma	skin	*epidermis*
duct	lead	*induction*
hydro	water	*hydroplane*
psycho	mind	*psychology*

SUFFIX	MEANING	EXAMPLE
-able	capable of being	*affordable*
-ness	state of being	*togetherness*
-tion	state of being	*generation*
-ment	a result	*enchantment*

First, Laurie does a mini-lesson to assess what students already know and introduce new information. She models Web-a-Word by thinking aloud about her process for unlocking a multisyllabic word, such as *automobile*. Then she asks students to think aloud with one another on a related multisyllabic word, such as *autoimmune*, because it helps them connect "the known" to the "new." She says, "It helps my students to hear how someone else unlocks a multisyllabic word. When they figure out one word, they realize they may know many more related words." Students use listening and speaking vocabularies as the basis for building their reading and writing vocabularies.

During the think-aloud, Laurie notes that the prefix *tele-* is giving some of her students problems, so she gathers those students at the back of the room, around a chart. On the chart, she writes *tele-* in a circle. She asks students to think of words they know that begin with *tele-*. She writes these words on the chart and creates a web by connecting each word to the center circle with a line. Students supplied *television, telephone, telescope,* and *telegraph*. Laurie added *telepathy, telekinetic,* and *teleprompter*.

Laurie tells her students that if they know the meaning of the prefix they can probably unlock the meanings of the other multisyllabic words. She asks if they know what *tele-* means, and together they arrive at "to send, convey, or transmit." With this information, she has students explain to each other how they might arrive at meanings for all the words. These are the meanings they give her, which she adds to the web:

- **television**—to send a message you can see

- **telephone**—to send a sound message

- **telescope**—to see something that is far away

- **telegraph**—to transmit a written message

- **telepathy**—to send a message by thoughts

- **telekinetic**—to send a psychic message

- **teleprompter**—to show the words in a speech

Laurie's students explored the root *-duct* (to lead) and created the web on page 105, with help from her and the dictionary. This web helped students see the relationships among words in a "family." It was an eye-opener for some of her students to learn that words such as *reduce* and *deduce* come from *-duct*. When one student volunteered the word *aqueduct*, it led other students to see that *-aqua* means water, which resulted in discussions of other words such as *aquamarine*, *aquarium*, and *aquifer*. So, discussions like these can have powerful, unpredictable effects on students' word learning.

Laurie has students work in pairs or individually to create these webs, and sometimes gives them as homework. When students master the more difficult prefixes, roots, and suffixes, she says, they have no trouble decoding and attaching meaning to the "Nifty-Thrifty-Fifty," words that include all the common prefixes and suffixes (Cunningham & Allington, 1999). The ability to recognize these 50 words instantly and automatically helps intermediate- and middle-school students decode, spell, and build meaning for thousands of other words. For every word we know, linguists estimate we can decode, spell, and understand the meaning of six or seven other words. So, you can see how knowing affixes and roots builds independence in word learning.

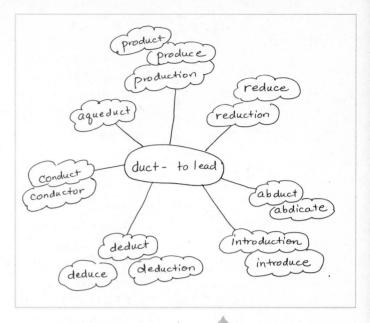

Students can see word relationships when they create webs like this one for "duct."

Nifty-Thrifty-Fifty

antifreeze	forgotten	prehistoric
beautiful	governor	prettier
classify	happiness	rearrange
communities	hopeless	replacement
community	illegal	richest
composer	impossible	semifinal
continuous	impression	signature
conversation	independence	submarine
deodorize	international	supermarkets
different	invasion	swimming
discovery	irresponsible	transportation
dishonest	midnight	underweight
electricity	misunderstand	unfinished
employee	musician	unfriendly
encouragement	nonliving	unpleasant
expensive	overpower	valuable
forecast	performance	

Laurie says, "Webbing words this way gives students an idea of the vast number of words that can be derived from one root, prefix, or suffix. Having them do it independently has prompted some students to explore the dictionary on their computer, and prompted some parents to buy a dictionary for family use. But, most important, I see carry-over into my students' reading and writing. They are much more confident in attacking and using multisyllabic words."

Another Web-a-Word activity requires students to use the dictionary to discover, record, and draw the multiple meanings of one word. By some estimates, 70 percent of commonly used words have more than one meaning, so this activity can be illuminating for all students. For example, third graders found four meanings for *spring* and created a web. (See sample below.) Other words to use for this activity include *bank, ball, rock, show, hot, second, table, pound,* and *down.* For more, look at

Use Web-a-Word to show multiple meanings of a word.

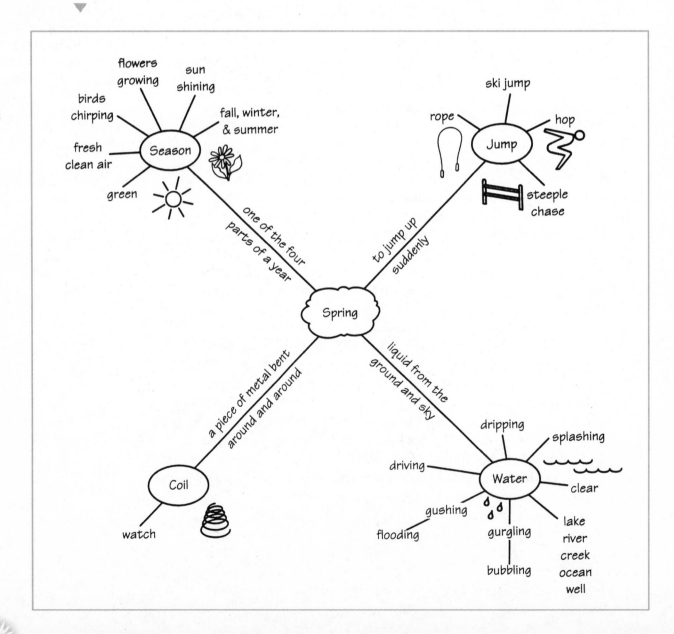

any page in the dictionary for words that have more than one meaning. You can also encourage students to investigate a word by creating and illustrating a web or list of related words, for example *potato* (*potato-head, Irish potato, mashed potatoes, French fried potatoes, baked potatoes, sweet potatoes, scalloped potatoes,* and so forth).

Word investigation activities like this work well when you divide students into groups of three and assign a word to each group. A triad usually has broader knowledge than a pair of students. Have each group brainstorm and then consult a dictionary to create a web as third graders did to represent the word *spring*. Have them post their webs on a bulletin board to share with the class and use as writing references.

A textbook or nonfiction book's glossary is another resource teachers and students often overlook. But glossaries are very useful. They are handier to use than dictionaries because they are located at the back of the book. Their definitions tend to be brief and easy to understand because, unlike many dictionaries, they are written at an appropriate reading level. Again, explaining the glossary to students and modeling how to use it are two good ways to alert students to its benefits.

Other important vocabulary-building information is often included in a glossary, for example, maps, drawings, endnotes, and photographs that can extend your students' word and concept knowledge about a topic. Here is a strategy that teaches students about the glossary, as well as other parts of a book:

◎ **A Book Walk** is a way to introduce and preview a textbook or an information book with your students. It provides an opportunity to give them an overall impression of the book's content, organization, and format. Begin by telling students that a book is like a sandwich. Then, look together at the slices of "bread" that are the front and back covers of the book. By asking students the simple question "What do you notice?" and listening to their replies, you will be surprised by how much they can predict about the book's content, organization, and format.

Focus students' attention on the front of the book: the endpaper, copyright page, title page, and table of contents, noting chapter titles. Next, direct students to the back of the book: the endpaper, index, glossary, and any other text features. Point out that the glossary includes technical terms, usually in bold print with a pronunciation guide and definitions, and then show students how to use the glossary and index. Lastly, look through the "filling" of this sandwich at the content of the chapters. Note how the author uses photos, drawings, graphs, headings, chapter introductions, and summaries, or other features that may help readers understand the content. During your Book Walk, try to use vocabulary that is central to the concepts in the book. That way, you prepare students to recognize the terms when they read and use them when they write.

Here is another idea to help your students learn technical terms:

Internet Connection

www.takeour word.com/search.html

www.word-detective. com/backidx.html

On these sites, explore the origins of polysyllabic words and many unusual words such as "blockbuster" and "gizmo."

◎ **A Glossary of Terms** created by students can build knowledge of technical vocabulary for a science or social studies unit. To make a glossary, select two or three terms from each lesson that are essential to understanding the topic and have students select two or three terms, as well. Talk about the terms, consult the dictionary or text for definitions, use the terms in context, and note roots, prefixes, and suffixes. At first, as a class and then individually, students can write definitions to include in their glossaries, based on the information they gather. Allow them to design their glossary pages and store them in their science or social studies notebook, or in a general vocabulary notebook.

To ensure your students learn the terms, encourage them to use their glossaries in a variety of ways:

◆ In groups, have students create a graphic organizer on the topic that shows the terms they are learning about and how the terms relate to one another.

◆ Have students write brief summaries of what they have learned, using and underlining glossary terms, and read them to partners.

◆ Pair students for a quick "Glossary Quiz": One student reads a definition to his partner, and the partner supplies the appropriate term. Switch roles with each term.

As well as providing opportunities to focus on words isolated from text, it's important to actively engage your students in processes that build words and concepts in conjunction with stories and text. Along with broad reading and writing opportunities, word-learning strategies that involve active processing by students are critical to good literacy teaching (Rupley, Logan, & Nichols, 1999). To learn new words and concepts, students must be able to connect them to what they already know. By helping students search their schemas for information they possess, you give them a place to hook new information. Connecting the "new" with the "known" makes the strongest link for remembering words (Johnson & Pearson, 1984). Here are some ideas for stretching students' vocabularies as they read and write.

Writing Poetry

Poet Paul Janeczko says, "Writing poetry gives you a chance to fall in love with language again and again." (Janeczko, 1999). It is also another way to play with words and, in the process, develop your students' vocabularies. Poets write with vivid and concrete language, often describing what they see and feel. So, reading poetry to and with your students is a good way to sensitize them to the rhyme, rhythm, cadence, and visual pictures that words can create. Then, set the stage for writing by engaging your students' senses—seeing, hearing, touching, feeling, listening, and tasting. Here are some ideas for getting started:

◎ **Words That "Sizzle"** is an idea for helping students find powerful, precise language to use in their writing—words that "sizzle." Mark Twain said, "The difference between the right word and the almost right word is the difference between lightning and the lightning bug." Share this quote with students. See if they can come up with other metaphors similar to Twain's that show how critical it is to use a word that communicates exactly what we want to say. One eighth grader I know came up with this one: "The difference between a bark and a yowl is the difference between flat hair and prickly hair on the back of your neck."

When writing poetry, it's a good idea to have students brainstorm their topic first and list all the possible words they might use. From that list, they can choose the words that best describe what they want to say—the words that convey as precisely as possible the image or feeling they want to communicate. Brainstorming as a pre-writing step:

- ◆ Encourages searching for the "sizzle" word that says exactly what a student wants to say.
- ◆ Sensitizes students to the nuances of word meanings.
- ◆ Stretches students' vocabulary and word knowledge.
- ◆ Leads to better writing because students are more likely to use precise, vivid language.

Another way to nudge students to think of words that "sizzle" is to give them sentences with less-than-perfect word choices and brainstorm better alternatives (McCarthy, 1998). Here are some examples:

Precise nouns:

1. He faced <u>a lot of hard things</u> bravely. (obstacles, problems)
2. They found <u>little pieces of things</u> from the meteorite. (rubble, gravel)
3. I've reached the <u>general idea</u> that writing can be fun. (conclusion, deduction)

◆ **STRONG VERBS:**

1. She <u>looked angrily</u> at him. (glared, stared)
2. He <u>looked very closely</u> at the moth. (examined, scrutinized)
3. The boys <u>called very loudly</u>. (yelled, screamed)

COMPARISONS:

1. loud as a _____ (sonic boom, bomb exploding)
2. slow as a _____ (sloth, paint drying)
3. pretty as a _____ (summer day, shiny new bicycle)

Once there was a stream violently
veering and swerving like a snake
slithering to catch its next victim or
vanquish an enemy
making small vortexes as it went
across a vast stretch of land.

Ryan, a sixth grader, uses "v" words to describe a stream.

Here's an example of a sixth grader's use of descriptive words that capture the speed and direction of a stream. It comes from an alphabet book of poetry that Joyce Lewis's students wrote as part of a science unit on water.

Here are three ideas from Paul Janeczko (1999) to help your students pay attention to the subtleties of word meanings as they search for the "right" words for their poetry. Each type of poem lends itself to using the thesaurus.

Acrostic Poems require students to choose a word, write it down vertically, and then craft a poem about the word, using each letter in the word. (See sample below.) Students can choose words based on a topic they know well—ice cream, skateboarding, pizza, football. Or they can use their name and describe themselves. Acrostic poems are easy to integrate into science and social studies; they provide a simple way for students to focus on key words related to sophisticated subjects.

Creating simple Acrostic Poems can lead to writing longer poetry.

▶

PATRIOT

People who are against King George
Americans who hate loyalists
Tough, they call themselves
Revolting is what the patriots called loyalists
Incredible is what the patriots say they are
Oppression is what they fought against
Terrifying, they called loyalists.

—Mary Skurski

◎ **Synonym Poems** are "couplets" that consist of two lines that rhyme. The title captures the subject. The first line contains three or four synonyms for the subject. And the second line can do one of two things: describe the subject a bit more or explain how the poet feels about the subject. Each line has seven or eight syllables, arranged to give the poem rhythm.

Vacation

Holiday, break, trip or rest
Whatever you call it, it's the best!

Machines

Lawn mowers, hair clippers, shredders, and sharpeners
Everyone uses them including carpenters.

Writing Synonym Poems broadens vocabulary.

◎ **Opposite Poems** are another type of descriptive poem, which are more challenging than Acrostic or Synonym Poems. They are two, four, six, or eight lines long. The first line is a question: "What is the opposite of…?" and the second line provides the answer. Or the first line is a statement such as "The opposite of…is…" and the second line describes the opposite by what it's not. To make a longer Opposite Poem, just repeat the first two lines and have students create a series of questions and answers or related statements on the same topic.

What's the opposite of ball?
Something that's straight—not round at all.

What's the opposite of kind?
Someone who's nasty and mean to your mind.

Writing Opposite Poems requires knowledge of word meanings.

More Ways to Help Kids Pick Just-Right Words

Don't overlook professional resources such as *Craft Lessons: Teaching Writing K–8* (Stenhouse) and *Nonfiction Craft Lessons: Teaching Information Writing K–8* (Stenhouse) by Ralph Fletcher and Joann Portalupi. Both books contain excellent ideas to spark better word use and lively writing. Also, check out these four books for grades 4 to 8, loaded with mini-lessons and activities: *Descriptive Writing, Expository Writing, Narrative Writing*, and *Persuasive Writing* (Scholastic Professional Books) by Tara McCarthy. And, you can nudge your students to use more descriptive words in their writing by providing them with colored paper, colored pencils, and felt-tipped markers.

These opposites include directional and survival words.

◆

◎ **Operation Opposites** is another strategy that focuses on antonyms. On a large sheet of paper, Paula Finch draws a web and writes the word *opposites* in the center as her students watch. Next, in each oval emerging from the center, she writes a target word. Her students then supply antonyms to the target word, and Paula adds them to the web. Then, individually or in pairs, students illustrate a set of opposites and write a "report." After students share their pictures and reports with the class, Paula posts their work on the web, near the appropriate words. Other opposites you may want to use include *first-last, over-under, ladies-gentleman, shallow-deep, expensive-cheap, inside-outside, thick-thin,* and *smooth-rough.*

Operation Opposites often prompts students to explore words beyond the target words. The report below, for example, shows how thinking about *front-back* helped these students think about other related words and apply them, such as *start-finish, beginning-end,* and *top-bottom.* This strategy is an especially good way to reinforce the directional and survival words that are critical for students as they learn to read, write, and take tests—especially for struggling readers and students learning English as a second language. And when two students work together, they bring twice as much to the activity as a student working alone.

Opposites web:

- Black & White
- Dark & Light
- Day & Night
- In & Out
- Up & Down
- Happy & Sad
- Left & Right
- **Opposites**
- Big & Small
- Top & Bottom
- Short & Tall
- Front & Back
- Hot & Cold
- Yes & No
- Cold & Hot
- Stop & Go

A student-created illustration for word opposites "Front-Back" ▶

front   **back**

Lots of things have a *front* and *back*. Rabbits, gerbils, books, houses, rooms, tv's, kids, computers, bicycles, dolls, and animals. But some things don't have a *front* and *back*. A race has a *start* and *finish*. A movie has a *beginning* and *end*. An ice cream cone has a *top* and *bottom*.

Using Literature

Reading good literature is a springboard to writing well. It can inspire topics to write about. It can promote interest in authors and their writing styles. And, indeed, it can stretch students' vocabularies. Two excellent sources of ideas for enhancing student writing with literature are *Lasting Impressions: Weaving Literature into the Writing Workshop* by Shelley Harwayne (Heinemann) and *Blurring the Edges: Integrated Curriculum Through Writing and Children's Literature* by Barbara Chatton and Lynne Collins (Heinemann).

Here are two strategies for using literature to explore words your students meet in their reading and may want to use in their writing:

◎ **Vocabulary Connections** is a strategy that encourages students to find a link between a new word in a story and a situation in a story they've read in the past (Iwicki, 1992). Use it as a pre-reading activity to introduce a word from a book you plan to read or as a post-reading activity to extend and reinforce understanding of the word. Follow these steps:

1. Choose a new word from a book you plan to read and display it and its definition on chart paper, the blackboard, or an overhead transparency.

2. Relate the word to a situation from a story you've read in the past. For example, you might connect the word *protection* in *There's An Owl in the Shower* by Jean Craighead George (Scholastic) and in *The Eyes of Gray Wolf* by Jonathan London (Chronicle) with *protection* in *Journey Home* by Yoshiko Uchida (Macmillan). The first two books are about endangered animals protected by U.S. law, the northern spotted owl and gray wolf. The third book describes a relocation camp established in Utah by the U.S. government, to protect Japanese citizens and immigrants from racist acts during World War II. Although the definition of *protection* is essentially the same in all three books, it is applied in different ways. Understanding the word in one context can make it easier to understand it in others. There are several variations of this strategy:

- Turn the tables by describing a situation and asking students to supply a word or words for it, for example, "I'm thinking of a word from *The Amazing Life of Benjamin Franklin* by James Giblin (Scholastic) that describes Ben Franklin and Paul Revere, whom we read about in *And Then What Happened, Paul Revere?* by Jean Fritz (Coward McCann)?" (answer: *patriot*)

- Have each student choose a word from a book he or she is reading. Write words on slips of paper, put them in a hat,

www.yahooligans.com

This site offers links to vocabulary sites related to math, science, and social studies. It also offers activities by theme such as exploration vocabulary, water vocabulary, wild arctic vocabulary, and Spanish, German, and French vocabulary.

and have teams of students pick. Challenge teams to connect their chosen word to another book, story, or selection that one of the members has read.

- Have one team describe a situation from a book while the other team identifies the words to describe it. For example, for *The Wretched Stone* by Chris Van Allsburg (Houghton Mifflin), one team might say "The captain is nervous. His crew is depressed and they don't want to work. They don't want to eat and they've come under the spell of the glowing thing in the hold of the ship." The other team might describe the crew with words such as *hypnotized, foolish, drugged, brain-dead,* and *addicted.*

Vocabulary Connections helps students see that one word can be used to describe many situations and, conversely, several words can fit one situation. It also alerts students to the fact that authors use different words to describe similar things. It requires critical thinking and memory skills as it builds rich word meanings.

Said Is Dead! is an activity Bridget Vavra, a reading specialist, finds works well as a vocabulary builder. She began to use it when she noticed her third graders overusing the word *said* in their stories' dialogue. So, she launched "Said Is Dead!" as a way to prompt students to use the dictionary and thesaurus and expand their options.

First, she and her students brainstorm and check the dictionary and thesaurus for synonyms for *said.* Then, they create a long list, which Bridget posts in the classroom for students to refer to as they write.

Then, she photocopies a comic strip with speech bubbles. Bridget uses comics for this activity because the pictures give her students strong clues to actions and emotions that inspire more precise and colorful words than *said.* She writes out the text of several of the bubbles below the strip, leaving blanks for students to fill in: "For the first time in my life I feel rested!"_____ Garfield. "How about some food, Mom?"_____ John. And "That's it! No more pizza after midnight,"_____ John. Bridget points out to her students that punctuation often gives clues to good word use, for example after a question mark, *asked* or *wondered* is more interesting than *said.*

Another way to build students' awareness of words beyond *said* (or any overused word, for that matter) is to have them examine stories, looking for the words authors use. Donna Powell, fifth-grade teacher, finds *The Bee Tree* by Patricia Polacco (Putnam & Grosset) an excellent way to show her students all the different and interesting ways there are to say *ran,* for example *chased, scurried, galloped, clattered, streaked, huffed, circled, raced, sped, sprinted, clambered, pursued, joined the chase, stampeded,* and *bounded.* Donna says Polacco also uses interesting synonyms for *flew: buzzed, swooped, headed, circled, dipped, soared, made its way out of sight,* and *led.*

Here is another example of two sixth-grade students who read different books and compared the dialogue in a chapter from each: *Saving Shiloh* by Phyllis Reynolds Naylor (Simon & Schuster) and *Holes* by Louis Sachar (Farrar, Straus & Giroux). They discovered that both Naylor and Sachar preferred *said* or *says* and *told* or *tell*, but also used other ways to convey how someone speaks, for example *jokes, calls, offered, confessed, declared,* and *muttered.* When they shared this with the class, they also noted that Naylor used the present tense and Sachar used the past tense.

Observations like these can prompt rich discussions about the choices authors make. And, when students make predictions about those choices, they "think like an author" as they become more attuned to how and why words are used, and the meanings they convey. Ideas from this kind of close examination often get carried over into students' oral and written language.

> Ch. 10
> _Saving Shiloh_
>
> Says ✓✓✓✓✓✓
> jokes ✓✓
> tells ✓✓✓✓
> Calls
> asks ✓✓✓
>
> Ch. 21
> Holes
>
> told ✓
> asked ✓✓✓✓
> offered
> Said ✓✓✓✓✓✓✓✓✓
> Confessed
> answered
> declared
> boldly asked
> Suggested
> muttered

There are many ways to say "said."

♦ ♦ ♦ ♦

SUMMARY

We know that "…vocabulary is the glue that holds stories, ideas, and content together and…vocabulary facilitates comprehension." (Rupley, Logan, & Nichols, 2000). And, we know that vocabulary grows when you explore words with your students in ways that appeal to their various intelligences. Investigating the meanings of words reaps huge rewards—you'll see your students' interest in words increase and their vocabularies grow by leaps and bounds. So, as a wise teacher, sensitize your students to wordplay, stretch their schemas, and teach them to use resources effectively.

Whether your students give themselves special names like Word Worms, Word Wizards, or PVI's (Private Verbal Investigators) as they engage in the activities described in this book, they'll acquire word-learning strategies that they can apply in their reading, writing, listening, and speaking. And, you'll enjoy the satisfaction of helping them get there.

References

CHAPTER 1

Ainslie, D. (2001). Word Detectives. *The Reading Teacher*, 54 (4), 360–361.

Beck, I., & McKeown, M. (1991). Conditions of Vocabulary Acquisition. In Kamil, M.L., Mosenthal, P.B., & Pearson, P.D. (Eds.), *Handbook of Reading Research*. Mahwah, NJ: Lawrence Erlbaum, 789–814.

Carney, R.N., Levin, M.E., & Levin, J.R. (1993). Mnemonic Strategies: Instructional Techniques Worth Remembering. *Teaching Exceptional Children*, (Summer) 24–30.

Bromley, K., DeVitis, L., & Modlo, M. (1995). *Graphic Organizers: Visual Strategies for Active Learning*. New York: Scholastic.

Davey, B. (1983). Think-Aloud: Modeling the Cognitive Processes of Reading Comprehension. *Journal of Reading*, 27 (10, 44–47).

DeVitis, L., Bromley, K., & Modlo, M. (1999). *50 Graphic Organizers for Reading, Writing and More*. New York: Scholastic.

Gardner, H. (2000). *Intelligence Reframed: Multiple Intelligences for the 21st Century*. New York: Basic Books.

Goldish, M. (1999). *101 Science Poems and Songs for Young Learners*. New York: Scholastic.

Hausman, G. (1994). *Turtle Island ABC: A Gathering of Native American Symbols*. New York: HarperCollins.

Hurst, C.O. (2000). Characters from A to Z. *Teaching PreK–8*, April, 76–78.

Inspiration, Version 6 (& Kidspiration) (1999). Inspiration Software. 7412 S.W. Beaverton Hillsdale Hwy., Suite 102, Portland, OR 97225.

James, W. (1890). *The Principles of Psychology*. New York: Holt.

Keller, T.S. (1999). Instant Pictures Help Teach Survival Words. *Teaching K–8*, 72–73.

Nagy, W.E. (1988). *Teaching Vocabulary to Improve Reading Comprehension*. Urbana, IL: ERIC Clearinghouse on Reading and Communication Skills.

Oster, L. (2001). Using the Think-Aloud for Reading Instruction. *The Reading Teacher*, 55 (1), 64–75.

Rumelhart, D., & Norman, D. (1981). Analogical Processes in Learning. In J.R. Anderson (Ed.), *Cognitive Skills and Their Acquisition* (pp. 335–339). Hillsdale, NJ: Erlbaum.

Rumelhart, D.E. (1980). Schemata: The Building Blocks of Cognition. In Spiro, R.J., Bruce, B.C., & Brewer, W.F. (Eds.), *Theoretical Issues in Reading Comprehension* (pp. 33–58). Hillsdale, NJ: Erlbaum.

Salembier, G.B., & Cheng, L.C. (1997). SCUBA-Dive Into Reading. *Teaching Exceptional Children*, July-August, 68–70.

Science Songs (2000). *The Mailbox*. Aug./Sept., 90–91.

Stahl, S.A., & Fairbanks, M.M. (1986). The Effects of Vocabulary Instruction: A Model-Based Meta-Analysis. *Review of Educational Research*, 56 (1), 72–110.

White, T.G., Graves, M.F., & Slater, W.H. (1989). Growth of Reading Vocabulary in Diverse Elementary Schools. *Journal of Educational Psychology*.

Winters, R. (2001). Vocabulary Anchors: Building Conceptual Connections with Young Readers. *The Reading Teacher*, 54 (7), 659–662.

CHAPTER 2

Beck, I. & McKeown, M. (1991). Conditions of Vocabulary Acquisition. In Kamil, M.L., Mosenthal, P.B., & Pearson, P.D. (Eds.), *Handbook of Reading Research*. Mahwah, NJ: Lawrence Erlbaum.

Cleary, B. (1963). *Dear Mr. Henshaw*. New York: William Morrow.

Dewey, J. (1938). *Experience and Education*. New York: Macmillan.

Harmon, J.M., Hedrick, W.B., & Fox, E.A. (2000). *The Elementary School Journal*, 100 (3), 253–71.

Harmon, J.M., & Hedrick, W.B. (2000). Zooming In and Zooming Out: Enhancing Vocabulary and Conceptual Learning in Social Studies. *The Reading Teacher*, 54 (2), 155–159.

Lawson, R. (1988). *Ben and Me*. Boston: Little, Brown.

Lederer, R. (1991). *The Miracle of Language*. New York: Pocket Books.

McKeown, M.G. (1993). Creating Effective Definitions for Young Learners. *Reading Research Quarterly*. 28 (1), 16–33.

Piaget, J. (1963). *The Psychology of Intelligence*. Patterson, NJ: Littlefield Adams.

Ray, B., & Seely, C. (1997). *Fluency Through TPR Storytelling: Achieving Real Language Acquisition in School*. Berkeley, CA: Command Performance Language Institute.

Rumelhart, D.E. (1980). Schemata: The Building Blocks of Cognition. In Spiro, R.J., Bruce, B.C., & Brewer, W.F. (Eds.), *Theoretical Issues in Reading Comprehension* (pp. 33–58). Hillsdale, NJ: Erlbaum.

Rupley, W.H., Logan, J.W., & Nichols, W.D. (1999). Vocabulary Instruction in a Balanced Reading Program. *The Reading Teacher*, 52 (4), 336–46.

Ryder, R.J., & Graves, M.F. (1994). Vocabulary Instruction Presented Prior to Reading in Two Basal Readers. *The Elementary School Journal*, 95 (2), 139–53.

Schwartz, R.M. (1988). Learning to Learn Vocabulary in Content Area Textbooks. *Journal of Reading*, 32, 108–118.

Stahl, S.A., & Fairbanks, M.M. (1986). The Effects of Vocabulary Instruction: A Model-Based Meta-Analysis. *Review of Educational Research*, 56 (1), 72–110.

Vygotsky, L.S. (1978). *Mind in Society: The Development of Higher Order Psychological Processes*. In Cole, M., John-Steiner, V., Scribner, S., & Souberman, E. (Eds.). Cambridge: Harvard University Press.

Watts, S. (1995). Vocabulary Instruction During Reading Lessons in Six Classrooms. *Journal of Reading Behavior*, 27 (3), 399–424.

Weaver, C. (1994). *Reading Process and Practice: From Socio-Linguistics to Whole Language*, 2nd ed. Portsmouth, NH: Heinemann.

Zivkovich, P. (1997). 3-D Words. *Teaching K–8*, October, pp. 58–59.

◆ CHAPTER 3

Avi (1987). *The Fighting Ground*. New York: HarperCollins.

Beck, I., & McKeown, M. (1991). Conditions of Vocabulary Acquisition. In Kamil, M.L., Mosenthal, P.B., & Pearson, P.D. (Eds.), *Handbook of Reading Research*. Mahwah, NJ: Lawrence Erlbaum, 789–814.

Conrad, P. (1991). *Pedro's Journal*. New York: Scholastic.

Gardiner, J. (1988). *Stone Fox*. New York: Scholastic.

Hesse, K. (1997). *Out of the Dust*. New York: Scholastic.

Johnson, A.P., & Rasmussen, J.B. (1998). Classifying and Super Word Webs: Two Strategies to Improve Productive Vocabulary. *Journal of Adolescent and Adult Literacy*, 42 (3), 204–7.

Palinscar, A.S., & Brown, A.L. (1988). Teaching and Practicing Thinking Skills to Promote Comprehension in the Context of Group Problem-Solving. *Remedial and Special Education* (9), 53–58.

Poindexter, C. (1994). Guessed Meanings. *Journal of Reading*, 37 (5), 420–422.

Rupley, W.H., Logan, J.W., & Nichols, W.D. (1999). Vocabulary Instruction in a Balanced Reading Program. *The Reading Teacher*, 52 (4), 336–46.

Vazquez, L. (1995). Guess and Check. *The Mailbox*, Aug./Sept., 18–20.

Weaver, C. (1994). *Reading Process and Practice*, 2nd ed. Portsmouth, NH: Heinemann.

White, E.B. (1952). *Charlotte's Web*. New York: Harper & Row.

◆ CHAPTER 4

Blevins, W. (1998). Make the Most of Phonograms. *Instructor*, December, 74.

Cunningham, P.M., & Allington, R.L. (1999). *Classrooms That Work: They Can All Read and Write, 2nd ed*. New York: Longman.

Cunningham, P.M., Hall, D.P., & Cunningham, J.W. (2000). *Guided Reading the Four Blocks Way*. Greensboro, NC: Carson-Dellosa.

Cunningham, P.M., & Cunningham, J.W. (1992). Making Words: Enhancing the Invented Spelling-Decoding Connection. *The Reading Teacher*, 46 (2), 106–115.

"Hit or Miss" (1998). *The Mailbox: Primary*. Aug./Sept., 110.

Hopkins, G., & Bean, T.W. (1999). Vocabulary Learning With the Verbal-Word Association Strategy in a Native American Community. *Journal of Adolescent & Adult Literacy*, 42 (4), pp. 274–281.

Martin, J. (1991). *Mitten/Kitten*. New York: Trumpet.

McGovern, A. (1994). *Playing With Penguins and Other Adventures in Antarctica*. New York: Scholastic.

Ryan, P.M. (1999). *Amelia and Eleanor*. New York: Scholastic.

Pinnell, G.S., & Fountas, I.C. (1998). *Word Matters: Teaching Phonics and Spelling in the Reading/Writing Classroom*. Portsmouth, NH: Heinemann.

Rogers, L.K. (1999). Spelling Cheerleading. *The Reading Teacher*, 53 (2), 110–111.

Routman, R. (1996). *Literacy at the Crossroads*. Portsmouth, NH: Heinemann.

Webster's New World College Dictionary, Third Ed. (1997). New York: Macmillan.

◆ CHAPTER 5

Chatton, B., & Collins, N.L. Decker (1999). *Blurring the Edges: Integrated Curriculum Through Writing and Children's Literature*. Portsmouth, NH: Heinemann.

Fletcher, R.J., & Portalupi, J. (1998). *Craft Lessons: Teaching Writing K–8*. York, ME: Stenhouse.

Fritz, J. (1998). *And, Then What Happened, Paul Revere?* New York: Coward McCann.

George, J.C. (1997). *There's An Owl in the Shower*. New York: Scholastic.

Giblin, J.C. (2000). *The Amazing Life of Benjamin Franklin*. New York: Scholastic.

Harmon, J.M., Hedrick, W.B., & Fox, E.A. (2000). A Content Analysis of Vocabulary Instruction in Social Studies Textbooks for Grades 4–8. *The Elementary School Journal*, 100 (3), 253–271.

Harwayne, S. (1992). *Lasting Impressions: Weaving Literature Into the Writing Workshop*. Portsmouth, NH: Heinemann.

Iwicki, A.L. (1992). Vocabulary Connections. *The Reading Teacher*, 45 (9), 736.

Janeczko, P.B. (1999). *How To Write Poetry*. New York: Scholastic.

Johnson, D.D., & Pearson, P.D. (1984). *Teaching Reading Vocabulary, 2nd. Ed*. New York: Holt, Rinehart & Winston.

London, J. (1993). *The Eyes of Gray Wolf*. San Francisco: Chronicle.

McCarthy, T. (1998). *Descriptive Writing: Grades 4–8*. New York: Scholastic.

_____. *Expository Writing: Grades 4–8*. New York: Scholastic.

_____. *Narrative Writing: Grades 4–8*. New York: Scholastic.

_____. *Persuasive Writing: Grades 4–8*. New York: Scholastic.

Naylor, P.R. (1997). *Saving Shiloh*. New York: Simon & Schuster-Alladin.

Polacco, P. (1993). *The Bee Tree*. New York: Putnam & Grosset.

Portalupi, J., & Fletcher, R.J. (2001). *Nonfiction Craft Lessons: Teaching Information Writing K–8*. York, ME: Stenhouse.

Rupley, W.H., Logan, J.W., & Nichols, W.D. (1999). Vocabulary Instruction in a Balanced Reading Program. *The Reading Teacher*, 52 (4), 336–346.

Sachar, L. (1998). *Holes*. New York: Farrar, Straus & Giroux.

Uchida, Y. (1978). *Journey Home*. New York: Macmillan.

Van Allsburg, C. (1991). *The Wretched Stone*. Boston: Houghton Mifflin.

Vocabulary Anchor

◆ ◆ ◆ ◆ ◆

(picture)

(word)

+ _____

+ _____

+ _____

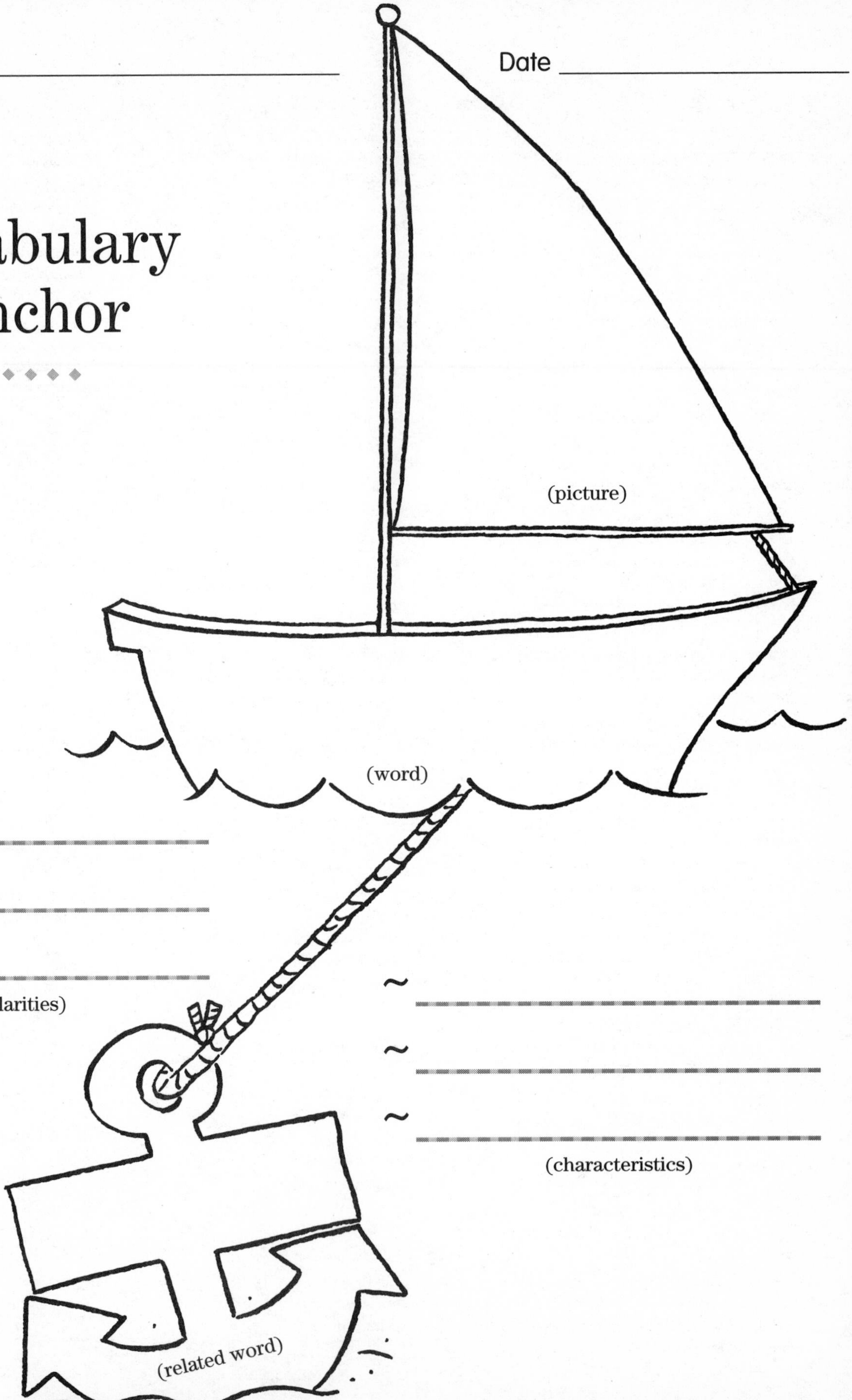

(similarities)

~ _____

~ _____

~ _____

(characteristics)

(related word)

Stretching Students' Vocabulary   Scholastic Professional Books   •   An explanation of how to use this reproducible appears on pages 11–12.

Name _____ Date _____

S2-D2 (Spell, Say, Define, Draw)

⬧ ⬧ ⬧ ⬧ ⬧

 Spell: _____

 Say: _____

 Define: ◎ Meaning _____

_____

_____

◎ Use _____

_____

_____

 Draw:

Concept Definition Map

● ● ● ● ●

What is it?

```
(          )
```
(category)

What is it like?

```
(          )
```
(property)

```
(          )
```
(property)

```
(          )
```
(property)

```
(          )
```
(property)

```
(  concept  )
```

What are some examples?

```
(          )
```
(illustration)

```
(          )
```
(illustration)

```
(          )
```
(illustration)

◎ **New Definition** _____

_____

_____

Stretching Students' Vocabulary   Scholastic Professional Books
An explanation of how to use this reproducible appears on page 41.

Name _____ Date _____

Zooming In and Zooming Out

• • • • •

Zooming Out...

6. Summary

3. Similar to:

4. Related to:

1. Concept

Zooming In...

2. Most important information:	Least important information:	5. What _____ might not tell us:

Stretching Students' Vocabulary   Scholastic Professional Books

An explanation of how to use this reproducible appears on page 42.

Name _____   Date _____

Interview a Word

 1 Who are your relatives?

_____

_____

 2 Would you ever hurt anyone? Who? Why?

_____

_____

 3 Are you useful? What is your purpose?

_____

_____

4 What don't you like? Why?

_____

_____

 5 What do you love? Why?

_____

_____

 6 What are your dreams?

_____

_____

Stretching Students' Vocabulary • Scholastic Professional Books • An explanation of how to use this reproducible appears on page 47.

Guessed Meanings

♦ ♦ ♦ ♦ ♦

Word	Guessed Meaning	Context Meaning	Dictionary Meaning

Stretching Students' Vocabulary Scholastic Professional Books • An explanation of how to use this reproducible appears on page 60.

Guess and Check

◆ ◆ ◆ ◆ ◆

Unknown Word	Clues	Guess	Check

Stretching Students' Vocabulary   Scholastic Professional Books   ●   An explanation of how to use this reproducible appears on page 61.

Super Word Web

◆ ◆ ◆ ◆ ◆

◎ **Sentence:** _____

_____

_____

_____

(word)

(synonyms)

(things that describe it)

(example)

Stretching Students' Vocabulary • Scholastic Professional Books • An explanation of how to use this reproducible appears on page 64.

Name _____   Date _____

Vocabulary Squares

◆ ◆ ◆ ◆ ◆

Prefix or Root   **Defined**

Definition   **Drawing**

Stretching Students' Vocabulary   Scholastic Professional Books   ●   An explanation of how to use this reproducible appears on page 85.

Name _____ Date _____

Word Tree

· · · · ·

Root Word

Stretching Students' Vocabulary   Scholastic Professional Books
An explanation of how to use this reproducible appears on pages 86–87.

Hit or Miss ❖❖❖❖❖❖

	A	B	C	D	E	F
5						
4						
3						
2						
1						

Stretching Students' Vocabulary   Scholastic Professional Books   ●   An explanation of how to use this reproducible appears on page 88.